WHAT TO DO ABOUT DYSLEXIA

ALSO BY RICHARD SELZNICK, PhD

*The Shut-Down Learner: Helping Your
Academically Discouraged Child*

*School Struggles: A Guide to Your
Shut-Down Learner's Success*

*Dyslexia Screening: Essential Concepts
for Schools & Parents*

WHAT TO DO ABOUT
DYSLEXIA

25 Essential Points for Parents

Richard Selznick, Ph.D.

SENTIENT PUBLICATIONS

First Sentient Publications edition 2019
Copyright © 2019 by Richard Selznick, PhD

A paperback original

Cover design by Kim Johansen, Black Dog Design
Book design by Timm Bryson, em em design, LLC

Library of Congress Cataloging-in-Publication Data

Names: Selznick, Richard, author.
Title: What to do about dyslexia : 25 essential points for parents /
Richard Selznick, Ph.D.
Description: First Sentient Publications edition. | Boulder, Colorado :
Sentient Publications, 2019.
Identifiers: LCCN 2018046021 | ISBN 9781591813002
Subjects: LCSH: Dyslexia. | Dyslexia—Diagnosis.
Classification: LCC RC394.W6 S45 2019 | DDC 616.85/53—dc23
LC record available at https://lccn.loc.gov/2018046021

Printed in the United States of America

10 9 8 7 6 5 4 3 2 1

SENTIENT PUBLICATIONS
A Limited Liability Company
PO Box 7204
Boulder, CO 80306
www.sentientpublications.com

CONTENTS

*Once again, for my wife, Gail,
and my children, Julia and Daniel*

INTRODUCTION

When children struggle with reading, spelling and writing, their parents often feel at a loss as to how to help and where to turn for guidance. Common questions that emerge include: Does my child have dyslexia? What is dyslexia? What is multisensory instruction? What does remediation involve? How is dyslexia assessed? Who should do the assessment? What is the school's role? What about private vs. special education assessment? How can we handle this problem? What are the implications for the future?

In over thirty years of clinical practice with dyslexic children and their parents, I've heard all these questions and more. Even though good resources are now available on the internet and many books have been written on the topic of learning disabilities and dyslexia, parents feel rightly confused and often quite bewildered. Additionally, many school systems are overwhelmed by a growing load of new regulations and edicts every year, to the point where they can barely handle the classroom struggles of dyslexic students. This only compounds parents' frustration.

In many ways, my first book, *The Shut-Down Learner,* describes what the educational and psychological landscape looks like for a child with a learning disability such as dyslexia. Since the book was published, I've been contacted by people from all over the world who are trying to obtain services for a child with learning disabilities, or who are just trying to understand those children better. I remember a mom calling me from a rural area of South Carolina. She wanted to get services for her child and didn't know what to do, but she lived in such a remote area with so few resources that there was little that I could do to guide her. Similarly, I got a call from a social worker on a Native American reservation – "We've got a lot of 'shut-down' out here," he said on my answering machine. I've also presented in Abu Dhabi and Dubai in the UAE, where problems with fundamental literacy run very deep and professionals need answers to some incredibly challenging situations.

Even closer to home, near Philadelphia, with its many universities and array of professionals, I see parents who frequently feel at a loss to understand their child's struggle to read, spell and write, don't know what services are available, and don't know what direction to take. Sadly, finances are often also an issue. Many of the kids that I've known or evaluated over the years haven't been able to get what they needed because personal resources were lacking to pay for either a proper evaluation or follow-up services, neither of which are usually covered by insurance. These parents have the same questions as any other parents but feel even more helpless.

I've logged many hours with kids who have struggled with reading, spelling and writing, so I've learned a great deal about the complexity of the issues. Each child I evaluate and each family I see is different, and I always have to take it case by case. But my overarching goal in my work with parents is always the same: I want to help them get it.

What to Do About Dyslexia: 25 Essential Points for Parents is meant to offer readers the same kind of support and honest advice that I offer to the parents I see in my practice. Just like I do with them, this book uses plain language to make things understandable and cut through the confusion. I'll never pretend to have all the answers, and I would never assume that this book is going to clarify every question that you have. But I can talk to you as if you were a friend or a relative seeking my perspective. I can try to help you maintain hope for your child while also staying grounded in reality.

The twenty-five essential concepts in this book weave through different categories or considerations. These include the definition and characteristics of dyslexia, how dyslexia is assessed, how to approach remediation, and other tips to help you and your child. This book isn't meant to be exhaustive. There will be more information you'll need to know and other questions that will come up as you continue on your journey, and making a list of twenty-five points will always mean that there are many more that didn't make the cut. But those that did are the ones I consider the most important for parents to keep in mind as they navigate challenging waters. They will help get you started.

I would also like to emphasize that this book is my point of view, my perspective. I'm not a scientist; I'm a clinician who has spent many years assessing and working with thousands of kids and families. I'm not writing to present a scientific perspective on dyslexia. There are many different ideas about dyslexia and learning disabilities and many different approaches to diagnosis and intervention, so when I give public talks about these subjects, people will occasionally challenge certain points and engage in lively debate. That's fine. I'm not invested in being right. I'm offering this information based on my professional experiences and my understanding of the research and the theory. There will always be other perspectives.

Lastly, before we begin, I want to note that whenever I refer to *reading*, I'm also referring to writing and spelling. As I'll

discuss in essential #5, these skills are all closely intercon-
nected, and for the sake of avoiding tedium, I'll often use *reading* as a shorthand for all three.

So often, parents feel that they are not heard or understood.
This book is the living room chat I would have with you if I
could meet each one of you. Even though I probably won't
have the opportunity to speak with most of you in person,
hopefully this book will offer you a little more perspective,
and you will feel a little more empowered.

Come into the living room and enjoy.

PART I

UNDERSTANDING DYSLEXIA

The Definition of Dyslexia

Trying to understand dyslexia or a reading disability can be very bewildering to a child's parents or guardians. You may find yourself feeling confused as you try to shake clear of some common myths, such as, "Dyslexia primarily involves reversals while reading."

The definition of dyslexia provided by the International Dyslexia Association (IDA) is used by most clinical practitioners, and it's an excellent definition for you to keep in mind as you begin to understand your child better.

The definition was determined by leading practitioners in the field, who arrived at the definition after a great deal of discussion and based on their best understanding of the research. They understood that there was needless confusion surrounding dyslexia, and ultimately they created a clear, comprehensive and usable definition. It has remained relevant for the thousands of dyslexic children I have met and assessed over the years, and it has helped parents understand their children's reading struggles.

Here's the definition:

Dyslexia is a specific learning disability that is neurobiological in origin. It is characterized by difficulties with accurate and/or fluent word recognition and by poor spelling and decoding abilities. These difficulties typically result from a deficit in the phonological component of language that is often unexpected in relation to other cognitive abilities and the provision of effective classroom instruction. Secondary consequences may include problems in reading comprehension and reduced reading experience that can impede growth of vocabulary and background knowledge.

To clarify this definition, let's break it down into its parts.

Dyslexia is a specific learning disability that is neurobiological in origin.

Some confuse the phrase "neurobiological in origin" with some type of neurological dysfunction or deficit. I don't like to consider dyslexia a neurological dysfunction or disability. As I interpret the definition, "neurobiological in origin" refers to the fact that it's hereditary, and in a vast majority of cases one or the other parent shares similar traits. That is, the dyslexia has been passed down to the child through a parent. While it's certainly possible that a child of two non-dyslexic parents can have dyslexia, it's much less likely to be the case.

Even if the parent was not formally assessed as a child, most will report something like, "Yep, I was just like that as a kid . . . I always hated reading and my spelling is atrocious." The primary traits that they share are differences in the way the brain processes information. For dyslexic children (and adults), these differences are a mixed bag of neurobiological strengths and weaknesses, which I'll elaborate upon in later sections.

It's important to remember that dyslexia is passed down because in many respects, understanding this point helps you to look at your child somewhat differently. Dyslexic kids almost always pick up on the underlying narrative that if they "just tried harder" or "paid attention a little more," their issues at school would just go away. It's been my experience that even the most well-intentioned parents fall prey to this type of thinking, which ultimately leads to friction between parent and child. A good understanding of dyslexia as an inherited condition that is neurobiologically based will help counteract the misguided idea that there's a motivational aspect to your child's struggles.

Dyslexia is characterized by difficulties with accurate and/ or fluent word recognition and by poor spelling and decoding abilities.

Here it is! If you want to understand the essence of dyslexia, this is the core concept you need to grasp.

One way I help parents understand this part of the definition is by explaining that dyslexia is reading inefficiency. That is, for non-dyslexic kids, reading is a relatively smooth and efficient process that is successfully learned by about third grade without too much special assistance or instruction.

For dyslexic children, on the other hand, the difficulty with accurate or fluent word recognition means that they develop a very inefficient style of reading that is usually laborious and challenging. In other words, they have weak decoding skills, which means that they have difficulty translating the written word into its spoken equivalent. Reading (including decoding and comprehension) becomes even harder as they move up through the grades and as more complex, multisyllabic words become more common. This is also typically around the third-grade level.

Whenever I talk to parents, I like to use relatable metaphors or imagery to counteract the confusing jargon that is often used to talk about learning disabilities. One of my favorite images to describe reading inefficiency is the image of driving down a road with many potholes: it's a bumpy, choppy ride.

To prove this point, open a book of your child's that you know is slightly above his level. Ask him to read it out loud without prior practice. If he reads the text comfortably and smoothly, then there is a lower likelihood that he is dyslexic. (Please keep in mind that this is definitely not the sole diagnostic criterion, but it's an extremely important consideration for the professional who is assessing your child.)

One other point to remember about the definition is that it says nothing about reversing words or letters, or about reading backwards. As we'll discuss in the next essential, the idea that dyslexia is primarily about reversals is a myth.

These difficulties typically result from a deficit in the phonological component of language . . .

This part may be a bit hard to digest, but it really isn't too bad once you start breaking it down. Mountains of research shows that language is not just one skill but is made up of many splinter skills such as phonemic awareness and rapid naming. Phonemic awareness is a term that you will hear quite often. It refers to the recognition of individual sound units within words (e.g., "bat" is comprised of three phonemes, b-a-t) and the way these sounds can be manipulated and sequenced. Rapid naming refers to the ability to rapidly label objects, colors or letters in an array. Difficulties with these splinter skills are seen to be predictive of dyslexia. These skills are what is meant by "the phonological component of language" and they are common contributing factors in dyslexia. Deficiencies with phonological components are at the heart of how dyslexics process information differently.

We'll elaborate on these phonological skills in other sections of this book, but for now, it's enough to know that they are subskills that, acting all together, make a child able to decode words and read fluently. I also like to think of phonological skills as parts of the engine, and when they're inefficient, they prevent the engine from running smoothly.

. . . that is often unexpected in relation to other cognitive abilities . . .

To determine whether a child should be classified as *learning disabled* for special education, many states rely on a formula that calculates the discrepancy between overall IQ and reading ability.

The IDA definition, however, does not use an IQ-discrepancy formula. The key word here is *unexpected*. Effectively, this part of the definition means the child has been shown to have enough cognitive ability – in other words, to be bright enough – that you would expect him to learn fundamental reading, spelling and writing skills successfully.

. . . and the provision of effective classroom instruction.

This is very important, particularly in the early grades (kindergarten and first grade). Some children show decoding/reading fluency problems early in their education, but when they are given "effective classroom instruction," they take off. Their learning curve is rapid and steep. *These children are not dyslexic.*

Let me put it this way: would you call someone *music disabled* if he never had a period of good instruction using appropriate instructional methods? Of course not. Before deciding that a child is not musically inclined, you'd need to consider what kind of instruction he's received. The same is true with reading development. A number of children in the very early grades are simply not ready for formal reading instruction. Before determining that a child is dyslexic, it's crucial to evaluate whether she has received adequate instruction and is developmentally ready to learn to read.

When a child struggles with reading but then takes off, I usually see two possible explanations. Either she was not developmentally ready to read before this point, or she simply needed a particular type of instruction that worked for her. In either case, if you provide your child with effective, research-supported approaches to learning how to read and she shows rapid progress, it's unlikely that she would be classified as dyslexic. Rapid progress is not typically seen with children who are by definition dyslexic.

Secondary consequences may include problems in reading comprehension and reduced reading experience that can impede growth of vocabulary and background knowledge.

This final part of the definition needs the least explanation, because if you're reading this book, it's probably because you've watched your child struggle with reading comprehension, wrestle with vocabulary words, or become frustrated over reading assignments. Your child is living with these problems, and you want to figure out whether they are signs, or as the definition says, "secondary consequences" of dyslexia in your child.

Use and Misuse of the Dyslexia Label

As is often the case following an evaluation, a parent will ask me, even after I have given him a fairly lengthy explanation of the results, "So, Doc, tell it to me straight – does he have dyslexia?"

While I think I'm very comfortable identifying dyslexia and have assessed thousands of kids with it, I find myself wanting to avoid labeling kids and reducing them to a diagnostic category. This is in part because, as I've mentioned, there are kids who have very mild signs of reading, spelling and writing problems, but whose problems seem to clear up nicely with good, focused instruction. These children were probably not disabled and labeling them so early on would represent a diagnostic false positive.

Another issue that I find challenging with the use of the *dyslexia* label is the fact that most people continue to misunderstand and misuse the term. If everyone used and accepted the IDA definition we discussed above, which clearly states the characteristics of dyslexia and the variables involved, then much of the confusion would be eliminated. But the use of the word *dyslexia* is highly inconsistent, and misunderstanding abounds in the schools, in the general public and even among professionals, as the common myths (such as reversals) are perpetuated.

However, let's say that we called dyslexia a "reading problem," "reading disability," "learning disability" or any other related term. What would the recommended treatment be? Would the treatment for a reading problem or reading disability be any different than the treatment for dyslexia? No, it would not. As long as the evaluator who conducted your child's assessment has identified the key points of breakdown (e.g., decoding, reading fluency, phonemic awareness), then the recommended treatments would be the same. No matter what you call the condition, a child with identified decoding problems needs good, structured remediation.

I think many people are comforted by the use of the term *dyslexia,* and giving the condition a name may help it feel more manageable. However, once your child's strengths and weaknesses have been identified, the more important issue is taking action.

Let's say that your child is struggling with decoding and reading fluency and the professionals haven't yet called it dyslexia. Unless this label will open the doors for him to receive services in school, you don't need to spend thousands of dollars more to find the one specialist out there who is willing and able to provide the label. Finding people who know how to do good, sensible remediation (as described in later sections) is a far better use of your time. In other words, evaluate to identify the nature of the problem and take effective early action.

Depending on where you live, this action step may not be easy. Even masters-level reading specialists are sometimes not well versed in the most effective remediation methods. And, as we'll discuss later, you need to be careful what kind of remediation your child is receiving.

Takeaway Point

As the first point on your journey, it's crucial for you to reflect on the definition and its components. The definition is workable and clear, serving to counter many of the classic myths and misunderstandings that I'll be talking about in the next essential. Sometimes you'll hear people say, "Well, we really don't know what dyslexia is." And you can say: "Yes, we do."

Know the Myths About Dyslexia

Our understanding of dyslexia is plagued by myths. How do I know this? Probably on a daily basis, parents come into my office and repeat them. I also hear these myths from other professionals. The myths run very deep, like grooves that have been etched into our thoughts. And once we start thinking in these grooves, we often have trouble getting out of them.

Here are the popular ones:

Myth #1: Isn't dyslexia when you read upside down and backwards?

This myth is the Big Kahuna, the Mother of All Dyslexia Myths. Ask anyone on the street what he knows about dyslexia and you'll hear, "Isn't that when a person reads upside down and backwards?" Shake this notion from your mental tree. Children, especially young children, commonly reverse letters like b/d, without showing the kind of reversal that people seem to associate with dyslexia. While I might see an occasional mirror image writing sample, the vast majority of dyslexics do not write or read that way. Inefficiency, not reversal, is a primary characteristic of dyslexia.

Myth #2: A child is dyslexic if there is a discrepancy between her IQ and her reading achievement.

As I mentioned earlier, school systems in many states classify children for special education based on a discrepancy between IQ (Intelligence Quotient) and achievement. However, when it comes to deciding whether a child is dyslexic, IQ is practically irrelevant. Regardless of whether her IQ is high or low, a child should receive appropriate reading instruction and should be subject to personalized, appropriate expectations for reading competency.

With that being said, one of my favorite tests used in an assessment battery is the WISC-V (Wechsler Intelligence Scale for Children-V). While this test does generate an IQ score, it yields other information that is more helpful to me, including language functioning, spatial thinking, problem solving, fluid reasoning, working memory and visual processing speed. With a child who has reading difficulties, the WISC-V allows us to look under the hood a bit to see what specific functions may or may not be contributing to the difficulty. By identifying the child's strengths and weaknesses, we can understand his problems better.

Myth #3: They don't really know what dyslexia is.

Yes we do. As I noted in the first essential, the IDA definition is pretty clear and operational. Dyslexia is not mysterious. It's a neurobiological, language-based learning disability that results in inefficiencies with managing the processes and tasks involved with reading, spelling and writing.

In addition to knowing what dyslexia is, we know why children are dyslexic. Although scientists haven't identified a dyslexia gene, and there are probably many different genes and genetic factors involved, we do know that dyslexia is largely hereditary and results in the child processing linguistic information differently than those who are not dyslexic.

Myth #4: Only medical doctors can diagnose.

While medical doctors can diagnose dyslexia, the only legitimate diagnosis can occur after a broad-based battery of tests is administered. Most medical doctors don't administer these tests; however, if an MD is giving that battery of tests, then it means that he is able to diagnose.

Your child will need to be tested in a variety of test formats and under different conditions in order for a diagnosis to be made. The required tests yield essential information about a child's phonemic awareness, phonological processes, language functions, word decoding, oral reading fluency, open-ended writing and spelling. If these functions are not assessed, there is no legitimate diagnosis.

Myth #5: You need to wait until third grade to diagnose.

There are plenty of signs and symptoms that start to emerge in the four- and five-year-old range (see the appendix for a list of common signs at each stage). You can certainly make very good predictions when a child is in kindergarten or first grade, even if absolutely definitive diagnoses are not made. There is

no gain in waiting. Don't worry about your child being labeled. Labeling is a smaller issue at this point, and the larger
issue is that your child may need appropriate early action with
targeted interventions.

Act early.

Myth #6: Dyslexia can be fixed.

Parents of dyslexic kids frequently ask me, "So, how do we
fix it?" This is one of my least favorite questions. We can understand, improve and modify. But since children are not car
engines, nothing is broken, so nothing needs to be "fixed."

It's important to dispel this pervasive myth and understand
what remediation can (and can't) accomplish – so important,
in fact, that I'm also giving this idea its own section as essential #4. For now, it's important to understand that dyslexia
can't be fixed, but it's possible to reduce reading inefficiency
and improve your child's skills through remediation. We'll
discuss remediation in much more depth in Part III of this
book.

The Weaker Language Functions Are at the Heart of the Matter

Often, once parents understand that dyslexia is a condition that is passed down through the family, they want to know why their child, specifically, has a learning disability. In other words, where is the problem located?

Reading, spelling and writing are complex processes, and there are many potential points of breakdown that may contribute to reading difficulties and learning disabilities. In the case of dyslexic children, there's almost always a contributing weakness in the language system.

If your child is dyslexic, you can usually identify the contributing weakness or weaknesses in specific language function by asking some basic questions. While I'll be talking more about assessment in Part II of this book, I'm bringing up these points now because they will help you understand the primary variables at work.

Here are some of the questions that I always consider in determining whether a child is dyslexic:

- How solid is the child's ability to perform phonemic awareness tasks? For example, "Say 'clip.' Now say 'clip' but don't say the 'c'." (phonological processing)
- How well does the child recognize rhyme? (sound awareness)
- How rapidly and efficiently can the child label objects or colors in an array? (rapid naming)
- How are the child's expressive and receptive vocabulary skills? (word awareness)
- Can the child interpret and infer from more complex language-based questions? (language processing)
- How is the child's word order when speaking? (language usage)
- Does there seem to be semantic confusion in the use of words when speaking? (language usage)
- Is there significant inattention when talking is taking place, such as in a classroom lecture? (language processing)

These questions are important because they each relate to a major part of the "engine" that is overall language function. If we want to understand why a child is struggling with the development of reading, spelling and writing skills, the language functions are primarily where we need to look. In a sense, they are where the action is.

Understand that if these questions reveal difficulty with any language function or functions, that does not automatically mean that the child has a reading disability or dyslexia.

However, each individual function is part of a larger language system, so any specific area of weakness will likely affect the overall development of reading, spelling and writing skills.

In other words, these functions are contributing variables.

These language functions also work in different ways. Some have a greater impact on the development of adequate comprehension abilities, while others are more specifically related to the development of phonological decoding and reading fluency skills.

Let's look at a child that I evaluated recently to help illustrate these points further.

Jamie, Age Seven

Young Jamie, age seven, is a classic example of these weak language-based functions in action. A bit late in developing her language skills, in kindergarten Jamie appeared inattentive during any activity that involved talking to her classmates, or during other verbal interactions like circle time. Always a child who seemed to have trouble finding words to explain things, Jamie also had trouble following sets of directions.

When more formal reading instruction started in first grade, Jamie appeared bewildered, looking around the room when the other children were asked to respond to different words put on the board or when they were asked questions about the stories that were read aloud to them. Jamie always gave the impression that she was one step (or more) behind the others in her class.

Jamie was not brought to the school's special education assessment team, largely because in spite of some of the identified areas of concern, she mostly received good grades. A lively, warm and helpful child who was a social butterfly, Jamie was immediately liked by her teachers, and the younger ones fondly called her "girlfriend."

One positive thing that set Jamie apart from other children was her elaborately designed, detailed and imaginative artwork. Jamie possessed an outstanding sense of color, and her drawings were quite vivid for a child her age.

However, Jamie's sense of self-worth was eroding with every spelling test and every time the children were asked to read out loud. She was frequently seen to be off task and described as "inattentive." The rating scales completed by her teachers also reflected this perceived inattention.

Unfortunately, the school over-focused on Jamie's inattention, and staff told her parents, "Even though we're not doctors, we think you should have her checked out further." In other words, the school thought Jamie had ADHD (Attention Deficit Hyperactivity Disorder), even though they could not explicitly say this to her parents.

Jamie was put on medication to treat the inattention. While she appeared to be focusing better in the classroom, she continued to exhibit signs of confusion when there was a great deal of language present in the classroom, such as when the teacher gave verbal directions or read out loud to the class. Also, Jamie's reading, spelling and writing skills were becoming increasingly concerning to her parents.

Jamie came to me for an assessment. As is true of many children that I assess, she showed higher skills in the nonverbal area for spatial thinking and other visual analytic skills. In contrast, she showed confusion in phonemic awareness when presented with sound manipulation tasks, and her sound segmenting abilities were on the weaker side.

Jamie was also quite inefficient with rapid naming tasks (e.g., naming colors and objects) and showed clear weaknesses with auditory sequences and following directions.

Her reading skills were also based primarily on words that she had memorized, but she was rarely able to apply decoding or word analysis skills. Additionally, her oral reading sounded strained and labored.

Even though I could identify areas of weakness and it was clear that her language functions were contributing to her problems with reading, the scores themselves fell in the lower portion of the average range. From her school's perspective, they would not be enough of a concern to take any action.

I explained to Jamie's parents that much of her inattention and difficulty with classroom activities was directly related to the areas of language-based weakness that were identified along with her reading inefficiencies and that her profile was typical of children who showed signs of dyslexia. A multisensory remedial tutoring program was recommended. This program would be designed to directly target her weak decoding and reading fluency skills, so it would also strengthen her underlying language functions.

Without this remediation, Jamie would probably flounder in the class, and the gap between her academic functioning and that of the average child in her class would continue to widen. Unfortunately, her skills did continue to decline, since they were not given the attention they needed.

Jamie's story typifies much of what happens when children show signs of struggling with underlying language functions. Virtually all children with dyslexia or reading disability have a number of language functions that are not up to par and are significant contributors to their condition. These naturally result in many off-task behaviors, which often lead adults to suspect ADHD when the weak language functions are the real culprit.

Takeaway Point

These weaker functions are strong correlates (common co-occurrences) with deficiency in reading, spelling and writing, and they guide later intervention. Talk to your child's psychologist or learning specialist about whether there are weaker language functions identified in your child's assessment and what you may be able to do about them.

Work for Improvement, Not a Cure

Why Can't This Be Fixed?

A mom said to me recently, "I don't understand. We've been at this dyslexia thing for some time . . . isn't it ever going to be fixed?"

While I do my best to be optimistic in tone, this is the message that I try to give parents in response to this common question: Dyslexia isn't an illness. There's no cure, and there is no fix like there is for a broken thing – because your child isn't broken. We all have our neurological predispositions, our natural neurobiological tendencies resulting in an array of different strengths and weaknesses.

If your child is dyslexic, then his central weakness is being able to efficiently master the skills of reading, spelling and writing. These skills can improve over time, but as Dr. Sally Shaywitz has noted, "Dyslexia is chronic and persistent."

Rate of Response

Of course, each child with dyslexia is different in terms of her rate of response and her learning curve, but my expectation is that as your child progresses through ages, stages, and grades in school, there are going to be new challenges.

The important thing is persistence.

A dyslexic child needs a great deal of practice with structured, multisensory methods. It takes time for the child to internalize the skills taught through these methods, so time is an essential element in mastering these skills.

The child cannot be rushed.

As a parent you need to be patient and satisfied with small gains.

This message is often frustrating for parents to hear, but it is a message that needs to be understood. Putting too much emphasis on curing or fixing puts undue and unrealistic pressure on the child, not to mention the person providing the remediation. Of course, it's very fair to ask questions about how the child is progressing and what the short and long-term goals and expectations should be.

Progress depends on a number of different variables. It's necessary to have the long view and try to keep the child emotionally connected and optimistic so she doesn't give up prematurely. That is why remediation (tutoring) must have a strong affective component. In other words, the tutoring relationship needs to be positive and encouraging, continually putting emotional fuel in the child's tank. Without this emotional fuel, it's much more likely that the child may become discouraged and give up, particularly as she progresses into the middle school years and beyond.

Takeaway Point

Trying to stay away from a fixing or curing mentality will help reduce tension and frustration. Keep an eye on reasonable long-term goals but have realistic short-term goals so you can maintain a sense of forward progress. Understand that even the best methods, followed under ideal conditions, still take a long time to work. And since progress does take a while, you'll want to make sure your child receives reasonable accommodations in the classroom (as we'll discuss later) in addition to appropriate remediation.

Reading, Spelling and Writing – A Package Deal

Reading, Spelling and Writing

Too often I hear people explaining dyslexia in narrow terms that don't do justice to the totality and complexity of the problem. These explanations largely frame dyslexia as a problem with reading.

One of the things to understand as a parent is that dyslexia is not just a reading problem. Dyslexia is always – well, at least 99.9 percent of the time – a reading, spelling and writing problem.

In some ways, the most challenging (and painful) aspect of dyslexia is written expression and spelling. In part, this is because when it comes to writing, dyslexic children are often thrown into the deep end with little support.

Rule of Thumb

Here's a rule of thumb to consider. Wherever the child is with her reading skills, her writing lags farther behind. So, let's say your child has been identified as having a reading disability or dyslexia and is ten years old and in the fourth grade. Her functional reading skills have been shown to be a low third-grade level at best, with total frustration at the fourth-grade level. In such a scenario, I would expect second-grade (or lower) level writing. As the child gets older, the gap typically widens between the reading and writing levels.

Just Do More of It

Schools have long held that children can improve their writing by simply doing more of it. This philosophy of developing skills through simple repetition drives many classroom experiences, and for non-dyslexic kids with poor writing skills, it may work fairly well. For dyslexic kids, however, writing is excruciating, and problems exist on numerous levels. They don't know how to get started, they're hampered by their poor spelling (even if the teacher has assured them not to worry about spelling), and they lack an internal compass for sentence structure. This lack of an internal compass is most likely related to their neurobiological weaknesses with language functions and to problems with active working memory, both of which are core components of the engine that powers our writing skills.

To illustrate how more is not necessarily better, let's imagine a common classroom experience from a kid's point of view.

Beth Ann, Age Nine

As a student in a regular classroom with no support, Beth Ann was painfully aware of her struggles with writing. Nothing was worse than just before parent-teacher conferences, when all the children were asked to write a story to post for all the parents to see. Some of the boys were as bad at writing as she was, but in Beth Ann's mind, they were just a bunch of idiots anyway. She knew that of all the girls, she was by far the worst writer in class. She had no idea how to get started. What did it mean when the teacher said, "run-on," "fragment," and "use whole sentences?" The worst was when the teacher circled every spelling word and told her to fix them. There was so much red ink on the page. Beth Ann could have used the computer, but all the other kids were hand-writing their stories and she didn't want to stand out more than she did already. It was just so embarrassing.

Need for Structured Intervention

Children with dyslexia need much more structured, guided writing instruction than is typically offered with open-ended writing activities. (An example of an open-ended prompt would be the classic, "Write about your summer vacation.") Open-ended writing is particularly problematic for dyslexic children, and using an open-ended prompt for them is the equivalent of asking someone who barely knows any musical notes or chords to play a piece of music. It's virtually impossible. Open-ended prompts should largely be avoided with dyslexic children until they have learned what is involved with writing a simple sentence.

Dyslexic children should get guided feedback and instruction on writing simple sentences and then progress to more complex sentences and ultimately to a basic paragraph. Such an approach is very different than an approach that uses "write what you feel" open-ended prompts.

Takeaway Point

When you talk about dyslexia, most people immediately think about reading and reading only. They may not realize that your child may struggle just as much with writing and spelling, may need just as much help in those areas, and that the open-ended prompts that work fine for other children may be your child's kryptonite. By broadening your understanding of dyslexia to include writing and spelling, you put yourself in a better position to advocate for your child and support her in the areas where she needs it.

Understand Extrinsic and Intrinsic Factors

There are many reasons why a child may have trouble with reading, spelling and writing. However, I find it helpful to put those reasons into one of two broad categories: extrinsic or intrinsic.

Extrinsic Factors

Extrinsic factors are variables that are outside the head. They are not neurobiological or innate to the child, and they may be situational or temporary. Extrinsic factors do not make a child dyslexic or give him a reading disability.

Some common extrinsic factors are instructional methods that are a bad match for the individual child and end up missing the mark. For example, it could be that the instruction is delivered in a dull manner that works fine for some children but doesn't ignite that particular child's motivation or interest.

Another curriculum-related extrinsic factor is level of difficulty. The material may simply be too hard, so that it frustrates the child. Far too often parents bring me examples of assignments that are clearly over the child's head, and no one, dyslexic or not, likes being handed a task that is beyond his abilities. We'll take the following case as an example.

George, Age Ten

George detested worksheets. They were so hard and confusing that they almost made him ill. The teacher gave his class one worksheet after another. It felt like it went on all day long with no real break. Then there were the ones that had to be completed at home. George had minor reading issues, but there were none of the usual indicators that went along with them. However, he shut down by degrees and became increasingly resistant to school work. Worksheets that were better matched to his level of ability and a better balance of teaching tools in the classroom may have kept George more engaged.

Intrinsic Factors

Intrinsic factors are the variables we consider when determining whether or not a child is dyslexic or has a reading disability. They're neurobiological predispositions, and as opposed to the outside-the-head extrinsic factors, they have very much to do with the brain. As we discussed in the very first essential, this neurobiological predisposition is inherited, passed down from one or the other parent.

I say "neurological predisposition" because as I've mentioned, we need to move away from thinking about dyslexia as neurological dysfunction or disability. Thinking about dyslexia as a predisposition rather than a dysfunction is not only closer to the mark, but it also helps to lighten things up for dyslexic kids. I believe they secretly harbor fears that something is wrong with their brains, and anything you can do to reduce that fear is something that you should strive to do as parents. To support your child, help him understand that he is not defective – he just processes information differently.

To illustrate how this neurological predisposition plays out within a family, let's take the case of Edward and his daughter Abigail.

Edward, Age Forty-Nine, and Abigail, Age Twelve

Edward, age forty-nine, is a photographer and videographer. For much of his life he has received a great deal of positive attention for his intricate and exquisite work. If you met Edward, you'd probably never know that he is also an undiagnosed dyslexic. Edward has done much over the years to keep others from knowing about this, as he has carried a deep sense of embarrassment and shame from his elementary school years to the present day. Edward is married to Linda, who does a great deal of work for him behind the scenes, like writing letters and emailing clients. Linda understands Edward's issues well, and she tries to compensate for him.

Abigail, age twelve, is Edward's first child. From a young age she showed a strong propensity for drawing and making various visual creations from different materials. In preschool and into early elementary school, Abigail was always one of the finest art students in her class. She also showed significant signs of a reading struggle from kindergarten going forward into the early elementary grades. Learning to read was extremely problematic for her, and she came home quite upset very often in first grade when others started snickering and making fun of her. Abigail had trouble distinguishing sounds within words, and she had no intuitive understanding of how to blend sounds together. By second grade she had fallen significantly farther behind.

When she was tested in third grade, Abigail was observed to have considerable strengths with visual and spatial skills and other drawing activities. Weaknesses were seen with her phonological processing, phonological decoding, reading fluency and sound discrimination. When the results were reviewed with her parents, Edward found them to be somewhat uncomfortable to hear, as they brought back many memories for him.

Abigail's case illustrates how dyslexia is passed down from a parent who also shared these characteristics when he was younger. Abigail is neurologically predisposed for difficulty with reading, spelling and writing; in other words, her dyslexia is caused by intrinsic factors.

Takeaway Point

Intrinsic factors refer to neurological predispositions passed down from one or the other parent who also struggled similarly in school. Extrinsic variables refer to instructional factors that impact the child's ability to learn. These can either be pedagogical (teacher-related) variables or related to the curriculum, such as poorly written worksheets or material that is above the child's head, placing her in a range of frustration. True dyslexia is linked to intrinsic variables.

Most People with Dyslexia Are Lego Kids or Visually Creative

My first book, *The Shut-Down Learner,* centered on children who tend to show high spatial skills coupled with lower reading, spelling and writing skills. This combination leads to discouragement and a sense of being defeated by school.

While not all shut-down learners are dyslexic, certainly a significant number of them fit the definition very closely. On average, dyslexics show a higher propensity for tasks that are more visual or spatial in nature. They excel with hands-on tasks. The boys tend to be what I call Lego Kids. Girls may or may not have a fascination with Legos but may demonstrate their visual and spatial skills in other ways (e.g., drawing, making crafts). Abigail from our last essential, who was always creating something, is a good example of how a high visual/spatial and low language skill combination may play out for girls.

As a parent, it's important to recognize your child's strengths because we can easily get fixated on areas of weakness, particularly when it comes to school. This emphasis on deficit can erode the child's core sense of self, leading to tremendous insecurity.

To help kids understand their strengths and weaknesses, I often use Howard Gardner's model of the eight different intelligences. I will show kids a list of skills, then ask them to pick their three best skills and then pick the ones they are not so great at.

The eight intelligences include: verbal/linguistic intelligence, visual/spatial intelligence, body/kinesthetic intelligence, naturalist intelligence, logical/mathematical intelligence, music intelligence, interpersonal intelligence, and intrapersonal intelligence.

More often than not, I find that kids do an excellent job of sizing up their strengths and weaknesses. The usual profile that emerges centers on spatial intelligence in combination with other abilities such as movement or interpersonal skills, depending upon the child's own individual pattern.

Take Andrew, age nine, who has been struggling to develop his reading, spelling and writing skills. Finding school to be an enormous chore, Andrew has increasingly resisted doing his homework. While no professional has officially labeled him as dyslexic, his mother has done enough of her own research to know with pretty good certainty that Andrew shows all of the classic signs. The school keeps telling Andrew's mother that she is overreacting. "You know how boys are," school personnel have told her. They've also made subtle suggestions that she seek the guidance of a medical doctor to investigate possible ADD, "even though we can't diagnose."

Andrew spends his free time in his basement making elaborately detailed Lego projects. He can do this for hours on his own with virtually no assistance, constructing Lego cities with towers and roads leading into each other. His parents are convinced that Andrew is destined to become some type of city planner or engineer, if they can only figure out how to get him through school.

Jill, age fourteen, is another example. While not a Lego Kid, Jill makes sketches upon sketches of clothing designs. Even though she's had no formal training, her designs have clear sophistication and suggest a future direction for her. When Jill isn't sketching, she's making jewelry for family and friends. Her designs are so good that many people have suggested that she sell her work on the internet.

Like Andrew, Jill detests reading, spelling and writing, as these tasks always leave her feeling so anxious because she knows she is terrible at them. The worst task is reading out loud. She always stumbles so much, especially with the larger words. Jill was recently diagnosed with dyslexia, which sort of surprised her because she always thought dyslexia involved seeing things upside down and backwards, which she never has. Jill was relieved to find out that some of her favorite actresses are also dyslexic.

Takeaway Point

A significant percentage of dyslexic children show a strong propensity for tasks that are nonverbal (spatial) in nature. These are the Lego Kids, the jewelry makers, artists and dancers. It's not surprising that a great number of actors and actresses, musicians and artists have dyslexia and struggled in school when they were younger.

Matthew Effects Are Powerful – Act Early

A number of years ago, Dr. Keith Stanovich published a very powerful piece of research that became well known in the field of psychology and education. The central concept of this research ultimately became known as the Matthew Effects, and these effects should be understood well by both parents and teachers.

The Rich Get Richer

Taking their name from a biblical metaphor, the Matthew Effects highlight the simple concept that the rich get richer and the poor get poorer. How do these effects apply to learning disabilities and child development? The best way to explain this is by comparing the experiences of two children.

Let's take a child named William as our first example. In preschool, William didn't encounter any difficulty. From normal exposure to the curriculum, he started to learn his letters and associated sounds. Participating in most of the typical preschool educational games, William enjoyed himself and did quite well. In kindergarten, the pattern continued. William started to understand basic word patterns, and simple decoding skills began to take hold. In first grade, William enjoyed the range of first-grade-level books, such as Dr. Seuss, which he started to read independently.

By the end of first grade, William was successfully progressing and everyone was quite happy. William's progress was self-fulfilling in that he received a great deal of gratification, both from the skills themselves and from the emotional satisfaction that comes with success. Put simply, William was in a positive feedback loop in which his emotional tank was continually being filled. By the end of second grade, William was devouring books. Exposed to thousands of different words simply by reading widely, by the upper elementary school grades William was solidly on his way to being a successful student. The smooth ride was enjoyable. Skills were developed on top of skills. The rich got richer.

William's classmate, young Marla, was his opposite. In preschool, whenever her parents tried to read books to her, Marla resisted, looking for anything and everything else she could do instead. Whenever the teacher led the class in activities involving letters and sounds, Marla felt nervous. No one noticed Marla's anxiety, but as she looked around the room, she saw that those letters and sounds were clicking for other children, but not for her. Any attempts at writing small words or even just letters resulted in embarrassing scribbles. She intuitively knew that she just wasn't getting it.

Moving into kindergarten and then early first grade, the pattern continued. When faced with reading, spelling or writing tasks, Marla displayed avoidance on top of avoidance. Compared to William, Marla was exposed to far fewer words, simply because she labored over one word at a time while William was already skating along. (Secretly, Marla hated William and she resented the other children around her who seemed to be doing so well, so easily.)

By the middle to end of first grade, Marla detested school, and everyone kept telling her she just needed to pay attention more. Any attempts at reading chapter books caused Marla a great sense of distress.

Negative Cycle

Marla's negative cycle continued all the way through elementary school. While she was formally diagnosed and classified as dyslexic by fourth grade, it was already too late to close the wide gap between Marla and many of the other kids around her. William had read many chapter books by the end of fourth grade, so he was exposed to a broad range of vocabulary, enriched language, and imaginative experiences, none of which were available to Marla. Bottlenecked by her difficulty, it was like there was a clogged fuel line in her learning process, at least when it came to reading.

As you can see from these two illustrations, the Mathew Effects are powerful. Each child's scenario was different, but both played out much like a snowball rolling down a hill. There is the positive snowball, in which positive experiences lead a child to seek more positive experiences. The child finds reading fun, so he gathers layers upon layers of knowledge and positive interactions with the text. Not so with the negative snowball, where unpleasant encounters lead to avoidance and to greatly reduced experiences with reading and exposure to words, ideas and concepts. With the negative snowball, avoidance is the most predominant feature. Although teachers and parents may think that the child just isn't focusing or trying enough, this avoidance really comes from the child's experiences of anxiety, shame, and frustration.

Takeaway Point

While it wasn't possible to totally prevent Marla from traveling down a difficult road, recognizing the Matthew Effects and understanding their power might have led to earlier identification and action, sparing her some of that struggle. Recognizing the Matthew Effects will not only help your child develop her skills, but it can prevent so much emotional scarring.

Dyslexia Erodes Self-Esteem and Confidence

Marla's and William's stories, discussed in the previous essential, also bring us to our next point. It's important for parents to understand the emotional and psychological aspects of their dyslexic child's struggle, specifically with regard to self-esteem and confidence.

About 60 percent of the population are like William: they get out of the gate relatively easily in the early grades and progress nicely in learning letters, sounds and basic sight words. In a relatively short time, in first grade, the decoding skills start to take hold. Before long, these kids are reading small chapter books, which then turn into larger ones. Reading skills progress along, as do spelling and writing skills. For this small majority, the development of these skills is as smooth and natural as other developmental tasks, such as learning to walk and talk. In my book *School Struggles* I call these kids the Smooth Road children.

The other kids, the 40 percent on the rougher road, struggle to a greater degree with the development of reading, spelling and writing. Depending upon other variables, such as family predisposition and their underlying cognitive functions, a significant percentage of this group are dyslexic, like Marla.

As we see in Marla's story, a dyslexic child's underlying insecurities take hold in the early grades and increase along with the growing demands of the classroom. While many develop very adequate confidence in other arenas, such as sports, dance or music, adverse classroom experiences chip away at the child's confidence. They are constantly looking around the room, making immediate comparisons between themselves and other kids, which leaves them with a mild, moderate or severe sense of insecurity. They become very unsure of themselves, and for good reason.

To illustrate this further, picture a typical classroom scene with Mrs. Freeman talking to her class of second-graders.

> Kids, you know your parents will be coming in next week for back to school night and we want them to be proud of you, so I would like you to write a letter to your parents telling them about some of the fun things that you learned so far this year. Try to write at least five solid sentences in a good paragraph and be sure to include a lot of details. Remember to write it in letter format, so be certain that your salutation is punctuated properly. You can write one sloppy copy today and then have a clean copy completed tomorrow. You will edit each other's work to help with the clean copy.

Mary Beth is in Mrs. Freeman's class. She hears some of what the teacher says, but misses most of it. She starts chewing on what's left of her nails. She thinks:

Mrs. Freeman is nice, but there is so much she doesn't get about me. I don't understand what a salu-what-ever-she-said is, and I don't want to raise my hand and ask. I know that my mother told me I should ask a lot of questions, but the last time I did I heard lots of giggling that Mrs. Freeman didn't hear. Most of the girls can write nice sentences. Their sloppy copies aren't even sloppy at all! My clean copy is always the worst of the class, and the teacher is putting them up. I know my parents try to help and they seem to understand, but there was that one time I heard my dad say, "Her work isn't even close to the other kids in the class, especially the girls." I hate it when we have to edit each other's work. The teacher always says we need to be nice to each other, but I know the other girls think I'm an idiot even though I'm the best gymnast in the class. I hate back to school night and putting things on the board. I want to stay home sick tomorrow.

In the classroom, this scenario is played out in some way or another every day for the child with dyslexia. There is an internal dialogue taking place, and we can only imagine its content. I am continually struck by what must be the ever-present stream of underlying insecurity that the child faces.

As adults, we gravitate toward our areas of strength, so we compare ourselves to other people who are on our level. Children can't do that. Since reading, spelling and writing take center stage in school, they become a huge mode of comparison. By looking at their reading skills side by side with others', children decide how they measure up, and dyslexic children must face negative comparisons on a continual, daily basis.

Takeaway Point

Insecurities inevitably arise when a child has a learning disability such as dyslexia. As is the case in most situations, conveying your own insecurities will be unhelpful, since that will only compound the child's negative self-feelings. To help your child cut through his insecurities, focus on conveying empathy and understanding. A statement like, "I know this is hard for you, but we'll get through it," can make a world of difference.

Dyslexia Is a Mixed Bag – There Are Strengths and Struggles

I've met thousands of dyslexic kids over the years. On average, they have a wonderful array of strengths, and I documented many examples in my first book, *The Shut-Down Learner*. Common strengths include a variety of spatial capabilities, creativity and a social spunkiness that is readily apparent. Dyslexics are often found among musicians, performers, designers of various types, moviemakers, architects and engineers.

If you can get a child through school, there is often good news on the other side.

It's important, then, for parents to try to strike a balance, keeping the child's potential in mind while also acknowledging the difficulties she will face in reaching that potential. I've found that parents rightfully worry about their child's emotional reactions to ongoing failure. The refrain from the parent is, "I just don't want her to struggle."

The fact is that with dyslexia, there will be struggling.

Often on a daily basis, dyslexic children are asked to do work that is simply frustrating and over their heads. This causes both emotional anguish and the anguish of trying to manage a task that is fundamentally unmanageable.

Nicole, Age Eight

Nicole comes into my office bubbling with enthusiasm. She tells me about her many interests, including her dancing and artwork. "I am one of the best dancers in my group," she pronounces. When we talk about school, though, her demeanor shifts. She speaks in lowered, muffled tones and tells me that she thinks she's not very smart. I ask why not. "I am one of the worst readers in my class – I hate reading and I can hear the other kids making fun of me."

Nicole's mother thinks she feels shame and embarrassment regularly. It's like she is two different people. There's the dancer self and the school self. They have very different senses of confidence. School really wears her down, though.

It's not uncommon for me to hear similar remarks from parents. The strengths and struggles of dyslexic children can be such a mixed bag that a child's confidence level can quickly soar or sink depending on the situation and the activity at hand. As Nicole's mother stated, dyslexic children can act – and feel – like they have two selves.

As discussed in the previous section, empathy and support are crucial. Be aware that your child is facing an uphill battle, and it will be difficult for you to watch him struggle. However, naming his strengths and gifts and giving him opportunities to cultivate and enjoy them will help both of you weather the educational challenges.

Takeaway Point

Since many dyslexic children have both great strengths and great struggles, parenting requires a certain flexibility of thought. Your child might be feeling normal, accepted, and highly competent at one point during the day, then ashamed, socially excluded, and inept hours (or even minutes) later. The parents who are the most successful in helping their kids endure the challenging school years are those who learn to be attentive to their child's changing emotional states and support her at both her low and high points.

Understanding Your Child with Dyslexia: A Recap

Before we start talking about assessment, let's pause for a moment to review some of the issues of importance for you as parents.

- We've broken down the definition of dyslexia so that you can understand some of the common myths and misunderstandings about dyslexia.
- I've emphasized that you need to think about reading, spelling and writing as a package deal. At the core of these skills are language-related variables.
- Dyslexia is neurobiological in its origins, and weak language functions are likely passed down from one or the other parent, who may remember struggling in school.
- The Matthew Effects teach us there is a natural process whereby the kids on the smooth road, those who are not dyslexic, have gratifying experiences that lead to more gratifying experiences in a positive snowball effect. Dyslexic children, on the other hand, find themselves in

more of an avoidance cycle. Act as early as possible, and don't wait to take effective action.

- Children in a classroom are continually comparing themselves to each other, so there's an inevitable underlying insecurity that impacts a dyslexic child's sense of confidence. Understanding and empathizing with your child will go a long way to offset the negative emotions he will experience.

PART II

ASSESSMENT

As parents, you will have many questions about assessment. These questions might include: who should do the testing (e.g., public school/special education assessment vs. private testing), what tests should be given and when should a child be tested. If private testing is involved, you may also have questions about finances and about insurance coverage. (Generally, insurance does not cover private testing.)

I wish I could tell you that these questions are easily answered, but unfortunately, that's not the case. In the essentials that follow, I'll be giving you some information that will help you work through the assessment process. But first, I'd like to bring up a few key ideas about assessment so that we can continue to fight some of the persistent myths and misunderstandings.

Variation in Approach

In a field like dentistry, for example, it's likely that over 90 percent of practitioners would agree on how to assess or diagnose a common condition. However, there's no such agreement when it comes to dyslexia. Various types of professionals may assess dyslexia, there are different assessment methods, and myths abound.

One of the bigger myths is that only medical doctors (e.g., neurologists) can diagnose dyslexia. As we'll discuss later in this part of the book, a wide range of professionals may be qualified to assess your child, but when you're planning an assessment, it's more important to consider the types of testing that the evaluator uses. The diagnosis of dyslexia involves tests that are designed to assess key areas of functioning seen to contribute to dyslexia. There's no single agreed-upon battery of tests, but research and clinical practice do highlight agreed-upon key areas that should be part of an assessment.

Quantitative and Qualitative Assessment

A good assessment must include a combination of quantitative and qualitative (informal) findings. I can't emphasize this enough. To explain why this is so important, I like to turn to educational therapist and researcher Regina Richards, who wrote the following in a small booklet she published decades ago:

> Dyslexia has been called "perhaps the most misunderstood word" in the educational realm. Why is that?
>
> The primary reason for the myriad of misunderstandings is that dyslexia is a language processing

disorder that can be manifested by a wide variety of characteristics.

Consequently, no single test or score can be used to diagnose dyslexia. Even skill in decoding (reading) cannot be used as a sole reliable diagnostic sign because with appropriate remedial assistance, 98 percent of dyslexics can learn to decode accurately.

(From Regina Richards, *Dyslexia Testing: A Process Not a Score*)

Even though this booklet was written some time ago and we now have the benefit of more layers of research and technological advances, the statement is as true now as it was when Regina Richards wrote it. There is a difference between a private assessment and an assessment conducted by the child's school to determine eligibility for special education, as I'll discuss further in essential #16. Too often, however, special education assessment focuses primarily on the quantitative, with a formula that calculates the difference between IQ and achievement score in order to determine eligibility for special services at school.

An effective private evaluation will recognize quantitative scores but will also include what is known as clinical feel or clinical judgment. This means that the evaluator can spot the qualitative variables that might indicate whether or not a child should be considered dyslexic. This clinical feel comes only from experience and does not involve scores.

For example, parents will bring samples of their child's writing for me to review. Very quickly, almost instantaneously, I can get a feel for the child's language abilities by looking at the writing sample to see whether it reveals signs of dyslexia. (As you'll remember from our discussion of the characteristics of dyslexia, I'm not looking at reversals as the primary indicator.)

When you're searching for a qualified evaluator, I would encourage you to look for professionals who are experienced in both the quantitative and qualitative aspects of assessment. Talk to the professional ahead of time. What is their experience with testing for dyslexia? What tests do they use?

Dyslexia Occurs on a Continuum

While people are often comforted by a diagnosis, it's important to understand that unlike other medical conditions that have a "Yes, he has it" or "No, he does not have it" quality (think broken bones, cancer, cavities, or any other black and white condition), dyslexia occurs on a continuum of reading/ writing difficulty. I do sometimes wish that dyslexia assessment was like an x-ray or an MRI, so I could give parents a "yes" or "no" with perfect certainty.

But, alas, no such procedure exists in this field at this time.

Here's how I visualize my question regarding the dyslexia label. Think of a bell-shaped curve made up of data points from many different children's reading assessments, with low reading efficiency plotted on the left side of the curve and high reading efficiency on the right. You would see many of those points near the middle of the curve and fewer as you move away to the left where children are less efficient readers. Now, where on this curve is the dividing line between dyslexic and not dyslexic? It's hard to say, exactly.

This is where clinical, qualitative factors come into play and are helpful in determining whether a child has dyslexia. For example, a child who is somewhat delayed and in the lower portion of the average range with decoding could go either way: perhaps she is dyslexic, perhaps not. However, if the child's parent tells me, "Oh, her father struggled with reading.

He always hated it and still does to this day," this adds to the qualitative information and to the overall diagnostic picture. It might tilt the scales in the direction of a dyslexia diagnosis.

Ideally, assessment involves a weighing of variables, putting information on one side of the scales or the other. This process ultimately leads to a diagnosis or to a determination that the child does not have a learning disability like dyslexia.

Necessary Components of an Assessment

Now that we've discussed some of the issues surrounding assessment, let's look at the major components that should be a part of any adequate dyslexia assessment.

Remember, while scores matter and they are a part of the assessment, there's a significant component of assessment that goes beyond the collection of scores. That is one reason why you should be seeking an evaluator who has a number of years of experience in assessment and who has seen a broad range of children or adults.

Words in Isolation

The first portion of the assessment should determine the child's capacity to recognize words that are presented in isolation. The list of words should span several grade levels, starting with a fairly simple list of high frequency (sight) words, or words that are very common and are typically responded to automatically "at sight" (e.g., dog, stop, run look). It should move on to more complex, low frequency, multisyllabic words. The child's response to the words will provide clues about the nature of her skill issues and the nature of her errors (e.g., vowels, vowel combinations, multisyllabic words, etc.). These errors offer insights into where the breakdown points are occurring in her reading.

With words in isolation, it's also important to listen for how automatically a child responds. This is an example of how a good assessment goes beyond the score.

Here's an illustration. Child A is given the following words:

- material
- possession
- institute
- philanthropist
- terminate

Child A reads them all automatically and efficiently, like someone might respond to basic math problems (e.g., 2 + 5, 4 x 2, 3 + 3). Most people respond automatically to words. But when someone does not respond automatically to words, that is a problem and it starts to suggest the possibility of something like dyslexia.

Child B reads the same words very slowly, hesitating and stumbling. However, he ultimately does read them accurately, so on paper, it looks like he has the same skill level as Child A.

Take Child B's reading of the word *institute*. He reads the word as "ins ... ins ... instate ... institute." It takes him about five seconds to arrive at the correct response. If the evaluator over-relies on the score and on the fact that the child did ultimately read the words correctly, the evaluator might then tell the parent that Child B falls "in the average range" and overlook the child's great difficulty in reading those words. This example illustrates one of my main objections to certain assessment methodologies that disregard significant qualitative factors, like whether or not the child has an automatic response to words.

Nonsense Words

Nonsense words presented in isolation may be one of the primary assessment tools for dyslexia and are the ultimate test of a child's capacity to decode. Nonsense words are extremely important because it's impossible to read them by accessing visual memory – decoding is the only way to do it. For nonsense words, the qualitative factors of automaticity and speed are just as applicable as they are to real words in isolation.

Some educators claim that the reading of nonsense words is irrelevant, as real reading doesn't involve nonsense words. I strenuously disagree. If you think about it, we are bombarded by nonsense words all the time in the form of names, which really have no inherent meaning, yet we are expected to be able to decode them. *Nordstrom, Ghiradelli, Patagonia, Wheeler,* and *Tahoe,* for example, are proper nouns that for dyslexics would be just as hard as nonsense words to pronounce.

Reading of Words (Real and Nonsense) Under Timed Conditions

The Test of Word Reading Efficiency-2 (TOWRE-2) asks a child to read a list of real words as quickly as possible with a time limit of forty-five seconds. The same process is done with the nonsense words. Since the test is standardized, it yields scores compared to others in the same age range. Dyslexics read words very inefficiently, and you would expect them to have low scores on the TOWRE-2. I find the TOWRE to be a very easy, yet powerful test to administer as part of a dyslexia battery.

Reading Orally in Context

Next, it's essential for a child to read some passages of text out loud. Ideally, the evaluator provides passages that start within the child's independent comfort level (the level at which the child can read fluently without any assistance), moving up to more difficult passages and ultimately reaching the ceiling of the child's ability.

Oral reading is crucial in assessing dyslexia. In fact, I believe that the only way to ultimately formulate a diagnosis of dyslexia is to listen to the manner in which a child reads. Fundamental questions that the evaluator should ask include:

- Is the reading conducted in a labored, word-by-word manner?
- At what level does the reading start to sound labored and strained?
- What's the nature of the word substitutions? Are the substituted words nonsensical, such as *viberate* for *vibrate,* or does the child use real words that fit into the context?
- Does the child sound like he is understanding the text, or does it sound disconnected, like he is getting nothing from the reading?

Reading Comprehension

Several formats are used to assess reading comprehension. A few of the more common ones are:

Format I – Word insertion in the text to determine understanding

In this format, the child reads a small amount of text, perhaps a sentence or two taken from a larger paragraph, with one word omitted from the sentence. The child reads the sentence to herself and is asked what would be an appropriate word to be inserted into the sentence. This format does not involve much active working memory, as the reading material is in full view the entire time. The following sentence, written at a simple first-grade level, illustrates this format:

There were many _____ that could be seen flying south for the winter.

Certainly, the child would need to be able to decode the words in order to figure out the context of the sentence. The Woodcock series of tests (Woodcock Johnson, Woodcock Reading Mastery) utilizes this format.

Format II – Informal Reading Inventory: Interactive with questions about passages read orally and silently

With format II, called an Informal Reading Inventory, the child reads passages at specific grade levels, starting with the earliest grades and moving up. In most tests using this format, the child reads a selection orally (addressing the reading fluency issue noted above) and then is asked to read the selection again silently.

After the silent reading, the material is taken away from the child and he is asked a series of questions about the selection. This task involves active working memory (recalling the elements from the story), and the questions are typically either factual or inferential in nature. Success with this format requires more language processing. There are a number of different tests on the market (the Standardized Reading Inventory, for example) that follow this format.

Format III – Multiple Choice/Standardized Assessment

Format III is the classic multiple choice, standardized assessment, which typically involves vocabulary and reading comprehension sections. The child reads the selection to herself and then answers multiple choice questions. Time elements enter into the assessment, as each section has strict time limits. Active working memory does not play much of a role in this assessment format.

All the different formats have their own inherent strengths and weaknesses, and it's important to consider the format when assessing comprehension. It's my belief that for a thorough assessment, at least two formats should be used. At our center we invariably include formats I & II and on occasion we will use all three. If you need to have the evaluator explain the format that she chose, don't be afraid to ask for clarification. If you would like to see results with a comparative measure, you can request those as well.

Spelling

As I've mentioned, talking about dyslexia as a reading problem is inaccurate in many ways. Since dyslexia is almost always a reading, spelling and writing problem, the spelling component must be assessed. There are many good standardized spelling measures on the market. (We use the Wide Range Achievement Test 5th Edition.) It's also helpful if your child's evaluator looks at informal samples that your child created as free writing exercises at school.

Written Expression

It's essential for the evaluator to obtain a good assessment of written expression. One of the problems, however, is there are very few good assessment tools, and the ones that are typically used (e.g., Woodcock Johnson, WIAT-IV, etc.) have significant limitations in their scope and the methodology used to assess written expression. As with spelling, informal samples of written expression can be very helpful. There are no scores derived from an "informal assessment." The downside of the informal sample is just that – it does not yield a score.

Phonological Processing

When you look under the hood of dyslexia, one big component you will find is a set of functions that are loosely called *phonological processing.* These tasks can be assessed with a variety of different measures. We look at these phonological processing tasks because they are seen as frequent correlates or contributors to dyslexia or reading disability. That is, they are likely to co-occur.

Here are two common tests that I also often include as part of an assessment battery for dyslexia:

Phonemic Awareness

To test phonemic awareness, the child is asked to add or delete a sound (phoneme) within a given word. For example, the child is told to "say the word *flat.*" The child repeats the word *flat.* She is then told, "Say it again, but don't say *f.*" (The correct response would be *lat.*) A more difficult example is the word *tiger* with the *g* sound deleted – leaving *tire*. For phonemic awareness tasks we use the Comprehensive Tests of Phonological Processing 2ⁿᵈ Edition (CTOPP-2).

Rapid Naming

As part of a phonological processing battery, rapid naming is often assessed. In this assessment, the child is given a series of colors or objects in rows and asked to name them as rapidly as possible. The RAN/RAS tests are very helpful and are used at our center.

Cognitive Functioning

Also as a part of an assessment battery it is helpful to determine the strengths and weaknesses of cognitive functioning. These functions include language processing, spatial thinking, problem-solving, active working memory and visual processing speed efficiency. The Wechsler Intelligence Scale for Children-5th Edition (WISC-5) is a good test for these functions.

Takeaway Point

There are a few key areas that should be part of an adequate assessment of dyslexia. Be sure to talk to the evaluator before the assessment to determine whether the evaluation will include these components. Dyslexia testing is not a simple process, and there's no one test that serves as the x-ray that will lead to a "yes" or "no" decision. A good assessment will involve many factors and requires consideration of both quantitative and qualitative variables.

Dyslexia Assessment – A Process, Not a Score

A professional assessing a child for dyslexia will certainly consider test scores, and those scores are significant. The Woodcock Reading Mastery Test, the Tests of Word Reading Efficiency, the Comprehensive Tests of Phonological Processing, and other standardized tests all yield reliable and valid scores, grade equivalents and percentiles. These scores can be helpful markers. However, the scores often don't tell the whole story.

Here's one example:

Jacob, Age Ten

Jacob, a fifth-grader, is in the 80th percentile of verbal intelligence and his nonverbal score is in the 65th percentile, meaning that Jacob's a pretty bright kid. Jacob's word identification standard score on the Woodcock was a 94, placing him solidly in the average range (32nd percentile), with similar word attack (decoding) and passage comprehension scores.

Jacob's scores would not have gotten the school too concerned about his reading skills. However, there's a lot of evidence in Jacob's assessment that suggests that he is dyslexic. Even though his scores are fundamentally average, he's very inefficient in the way that he reads. For example, while he read words like *institute* and *mechanic* correctly, it took him a great deal of effort. It was hard for Jacob to figure out the words. For kids who are not dyslexic, word reading is smooth and effortless. Those words would be a piece of cake for non-dyslexic fifth-graders.

Then there was the way that Jacob read passages out loud. Listening to him read was almost painful. Every time he came to a large word that's not all that common (like *hysterical, pedestrian* or *departure),* he hesitated for a few seconds and either stumbled on the right word or substituted one that made no sense – like substituting *ostrich* for *orchestra.* The substitution completely changed the meaning. Another example is that when reading a line from a story that said, "He hid his boat in *seaweed,*" Jacob read this as, "He hid his boat in *Sweden.*"

Finally, the two other areas of concern were Jacob's writing and his spelling. While he could memorize for the spelling test, his spelling and his open-ended writing were very weak. The amount of effort he put into writing a small informal paragraph was considerable. There also wasn't one sentence that was complete.

Here are some of Jacob's spelling errors and the way that he completed a paragraph in response to a prompt that was given to him:

- make/mack
- dress/des

- will/whill
- outside/otsid
- ruin/rune
- brief/breef
- executive/exutive

Prompt I

    One Day a girl was on a tirer swinge and she did not see her dog was at the winedow. the dog wanted to go out side with the gril. The gril finly saw her dog and let the dog outside.

Prompt II

    When I grow uo I want to be a enganeer Being a enganeer is a fun job becase you get to bild stuff. But it will Be a hard job becase when stuff brakes they have to fix it. You need a lot of tools to be a enganeer you have to worck hard. I want to be a enganeer because my dad is one and his dad is one. A enganeer is good at math. I love to bild like my dad. I relly want to be a enganeer. It sounds so much fun. Some day I want to be a enganeer like my dad. I like to bild But it is hard to bild.

Even though Jacob is unlikely to be classified eligible for special education, I think he has a learning disability that matches the clinical definition of dyslexia.

With a kid like Jacob, his assessment scores simply don't tell the whole story. To figure out what's going on under the hood that's causing his reading struggles, I had to watch him read and make a number of those qualitative observations that we discussed in the last essential.

If you take your child for a private assessment, be sure to talk about the qualitative signs or the clinical observations that were noted and observed. How was the reading conducted? Was it strained and laborious? Word-by-word? Insecure? Slow and hesitant? Even if your child's scores are roughly average, these questions and others like them might determine whether there is another side to the story.

This discussion of test scores and their limitations leads me to an important point that we need to clarify – and a myth we need to dispel – before we continue in our discussion of assessment.

Takeaway Point

Scores are helpful and necessary as a part of any evaluation, whether done privately or in the public schools. However, they cannot tell the whole story, as I've illustrated in a number of different places in this text. Observations and clinical feel are as much a part of an assessment as the test scores. As Regina Richards said many years ago, "Dyslexia testing is a process, not a score." Or, as I've said before, there is no dyslexia x-ray.

ESSENTIAL #13

Finding the Right Evaluator

In our essential about dyslexia myths, I briefly touched on one persistent misconception: that since dyslexia is a medical condition, only medical doctors (typically neurologists) are qualified to do the assessment or offer a diagnosis of dyslexia. I would like to elaborate on this point.

Neurologists can certainly provide a biomedical view of your child's condition. They can give helpful commentary on whether there are any gross neurological concerns or even minimal neurological dysfunction. However, a neurological assessment rarely involves the battery of tests necessary to assess dyslexia. In fact, over the years, I've personally known only one medical doctor who did a broad-based neurodevelopmental assessment covering a number of those key areas. Practitioners like him are something of a rarity in the medical field.

A typical neurological consultation goes something like this. It lasts between thirty and forty-five minutes, and if it's the first visit (and often this is the only visit), the first half of the consultation will be devoted to a clinical interview with the parents to clarify the problem and obtain a detailed history. The next fifteen minutes or so has the child going through a variety of neurological function screening tasks, such as tapping each finger rapidly to the thumb in succession, walking a straight line, tracking a visual field, and other fine and gross motor activities. Some neurologists may have the child write their name and copy a series of symbols using paper and pencil. The purpose of these tasks is to screen for any neurological irregularities.

Not Part of a Typical Neurological Examination

The following tasks – which are all essential to assessment of dyslexia – are not part of a typical neurological examination:

- Reading from a graded word list to determine word identification adequacy and level of automatic word reading response.
- Reading real and nonsense words in isolation under timed conditions.
- Reading aloud passages at specific grade levels and under standard conditions to determine reading accuracy, reading fluency and oral reading competence.
- Spelling of real and nonsense words.
- Writing a paragraph.
- Screenings of phonological processing competence, including phonemic awareness and measure of rapid automatic naming.
- Perceptual screenings including copying a series of increasingly difficult geometric designs.
- Screenings of language functions.

Since the way that a child responds to words and passages of text is the primary means of determining dyslexia, and since it's also key to consider spelling and writing, these elements must be included in any competent assessment.

The assessments listed above would probably require the evaluator to spend at least an hour and a half to two hours of face time with the child, not to mention the time spent scoring, interpreting and writing up the results. Not to be at all critical of MDs, who have many areas of expertise, but this type of testing is just not usually one of them. The timeframe of a typical pediatric neurological screening is also too short to accommodate the necessary assessment components for dyslexia. In fact, if you received a "diagnosis" just on the basis of a pediatric neurological examination, certain pieces of valuable information would invariably be missing.

Choosing an Evaluator

If a neurologist isn't necessarily the best person to assess your child, then who is?

I'm partial to psychologists (including school psychologists) and neuropsychologists for most types of dyslexia assessment, as they're usually very well versed in the relevant assessment areas. However, it's also important to understand that many psychologists know virtually nothing about learning disabilities and dyslexia because they specialize in other areas and conditions. For example, a psychologist who specializes in the treatment of eating disorders or marriage therapy will probably not be qualified. If you're looking for a psychologist to assess your child, be sure to look for someone who has specific experience with learning disabilities.

Reading/learning specialists and other special educators who do this type of testing are also worth considering, as they often have solid experience in assessing a broad range of critical areas.

Speech and language professionals and specialists in auditory processing may also be helpful, but they typically use a narrower band of assessment tools that are more tailored to their specialty.

How do you choose a specific evaluator? There are a number of different considerations, but word-of-mouth referral is often a good place to start. I would also ask your pediatrician to offer some suggestions, as pediatricians usually know which professionals in the community have good reputations.

Takeaway Point

If dyslexia or learning disabilities are your primary concern, going to a medical doctor for an assessment may not be your best move. There is a battery of tests that are essential in assessing dyslexia, and they are simply not in the purview of neurologists or other medical doctors. Also, be aware that each state may have its own regulations or guidelines about who can diagnose. For example, some states specify that only school psychologists or neuropsychologists can diagnose dyslexia.

Understanding Active Working Memory

As we discussed earlier, there are several common correlates of dyslexia. We can think of these as predictors indicating the likelihood that your child will have dyslexia. When a child does well with one of the correlates, we can predict that she will end up reading, spelling and writing adequately. Conversely, when a child does poorly on some of the correlates, then she is less likely to develop adequate reading, spelling and writing skills.

Here's a helpful parallel: eating certain foods and exercising frequently are correlated with good cardiovascular conditioning and overall health. Of course, you can have wonderful eating habits and still have poor health, or you may exercise regularly and still have a cardiac condition. But good diet, good exercise, and good cardiovascular health are likely to go together. The word *likely* is very important. Exercising likely co-occurs with good cardiovascular health, but it certainly does not guarantee it.

Good Active Working Memory (AWM) likely co-occurs with good performance on language tasks, such as the processes involved with reading, spelling and writing. AWM allows us to do a sort of internal juggling of different memories to carry out a task. I like to think of working memory as somewhat similar to another acronym you might be familiar with – the Random Access Memory (RAM) on a computer.

The more RAM you have, the more efficient the computer. The more active working memory you have, the more efficient your cognitive functioning and processing will be. This is especially the case with auditory sequential memory, which is one of the subskills of AWM and is an especially strong correlate of language tasks.

Classic Active Working Memory Tasks

What are some classic AWM tasks, and how would we test your child's performance on those? In a dyslexia assessment battery you would look to tasks such as digit span, letter number sequencing and arithmetic as signs of adequate AWM function.

Digit Span

In a digit span test, the child is presented with a series of numbers – let's say, 3-9-6-1-7 – and asked to repeat them back. Then the child is given another series (4-6-2-7) and asked to repeat it in reverse order (so the correct response would be 7-2-6-4). This latter aspect of digit span, the recall of digits in a reversed order, is particularly problematic for people with dyslexia or other reading disabilities. I've found reverse digit span to be an extremely sensitive indicator:

trouble with this task will likely co-occur with decoding and spelling problems.

Also within a digit span task, children are often asked to put numbers in a proper sequence. So if they were presented with 9-4-6-3, the answer would be 3-4-6-9.

The numerical score you'll receive for the digit span test covers the whole thing, forward and reverse, so the score may not tell the whole story. For this reason, you should ask your child's evaluator about how your child performed specifically on the different components of the digit span task.

Letter-Number Sequencing

This is another task from the psychological test battery that is a sensitive indicator for issues of active working memory, specifically auditory processing. In this task, the child is given a random string of letters and numbers out loud and asked to say the string back with the numbers first and then the letters, each in proper ascending order. So, if the string is B-1-2-J, the answer would be 1-2-B-J.

Arithmetic

The final member of this triad of auditory active working memory tasks is the arithmetic subtest (although this subtest is not formally included in the active working memory factor on the WISC-V). The child is given a spoken arithmetic word problem to solve, and they are not allowed to read or write down the problem.

An example would be, "Bill, Dave and Tom each earned 9 dollars working in a supermarket. How much did they earn all together?" Under the rules of this test, the evaluator is allowed to repeat the question one time.

This auditory word problem illustrates how AWM or auditory sequential recall comes into play in our everyday lives. Given information in the form of language, we are required to make calculations and decisions. Children use AWM when they are asked to follow directions, and many parents of dyslexic children report that their kids do not follow directions well. Adults often wrongly assume that this is because the child has ADHD or ADD, when in fact it's a weakness in the language system that is preventing him from efficiently processing information.

If your child has been evaluated, pull out the psychological portion of the assessment and look for the section of the WISC-V that references active working memory. Are the scores below the midpoint (below 10)? Did the evaluator make comments on the results of the active working memory tasks? If so, then it's likely that AWM is a factor in your child's dyslexia diagnosis.

Takeaway Point

The main thing to remember about AWM is that it's enormously important as a correlate or a predictor of dyslexia. When a child does poorly on AWM tasks, they will likely do poorly on tasks involving phonological decoding, reading fluency, spelling and writing.

If you think this may be the case for your child, then after she has been assessed, talk with the consultant or psychologist who did the testing. Ask them specifically how she did with these tasks and what the numbers mean. Her performance on these tests will help give you perspective on the underlying issues. There are no agreed-upon fixes for active working memory problems, but there are basic mindsets that parents can bring to their interactions with their child. First and foremost is being patient with her when she has trouble keeping sequential information straight. Be ready to stop and back up. Help her with directions. Consider putting directions in some visual form, if possible.

The Name Game Explains Phonemic Awareness

There are many terms within the field of learning disabilities and education psychology that don't translate very well. My criteria for determining whether something is translating well is the person-on-the-street standard: if you stopped the average person on the street and asked him what a term means, and he just gave you a confused look, then the term is probably jargon. *Phonemic awareness* is one such term. It doesn't translate well, and it's not readily understood. I like to explain it, then, by talking about the Name Game.

The Name Game was a popular song back in the 1960s. Most adults and many children still know this song nowadays, but if you don't, it's worth finding and listening to the song a few times, then try it with your child.

The Name Game starts with a person's name, then involves rhyming and dropping and adding sounds to words in a playful fashion. For the name *Shannon,* it goes something like this:

Shannon Shannon bo Bannon
Banana fana fo Fannon
Fee fi mo Mannon
Shannon

Phonemic awareness essentially means the awareness of sound, including the manipulation of sounds within words. The Name Game, with its rhyming and sound substitutions, is a vigorous exercise in phonemic awareness. For children who don't have trouble with this language skill, the Name Game is a piece of cake, and since singing along is a lively, interactive activity, most young children love it. However, for children who encounter difficulty with awareness of sounds and struggle with the subtleties involved with rhyming and sound manipulation, the Name Game is usually challenging. Since phonemic awareness overlaps with early decoding skills, children who have trouble with the Name Game are likely to struggle with decoding, as well.

Takeaway Point

Very early in a child's development, we can find some indicators that predict who is likely to struggle in the development of their basic reading, spelling and writing skills. The terms *phonemic awareness* or *phonological processing* can be bewildering to parents, but using the Name Game as an example of phonemic awareness or phonological processing in action can help you understand what's going on with your child.

Private Assessment and Special Education Assessment

As we touched on in the overview, one thing to think about when planning for your child's assessment is the difference between a special education assessment completed by the school and a private assessment. There are advantages and disadvantages to each, in terms of how the assessment is conducted and what information it will provide about your child's problems. The sooner you understand the distinctions and the differences between the two, the better. It will save you a great deal of frustration and confusion.

Special Education Classification vs. Dyslexia Diagnosis

It can be quite confusing for parents when they see their child struggle on a daily basis, but he is assessed as ineligible for special education services. In my experience, it is not only possible but very common for a child to be diagnosed as dyslexic by a non-school professional but then found to be ineligible for special education services. This is the case because special education assessment has one primary purpose, and that is to determine whether a child is eligible for special education through the school. Special education classification is almost entirely based on the numerical scores derived in an assessment.

If the special education team at a child's school does determine that the child is eligible for services, this means that the team has found sufficient evidence to classify the child as "handicapped" or "disabled." Once this classification is made, the school must create an IEP (Individualized Education Plan) specifically for this child.

Contrast this with the purpose of a private assessment, which is to evaluate a number of different areas of a child's functioning and, depending on the findings, possibly issue a diagnosis of dyslexia or a learning disability. The professional making the diagnosis will consider scores but also draw from clinical observations, which in many ways are more revealing and informative.

I'd like to emphasize this point for a moment: parents' feelings about this "disabled" or "handicapped" classification, or dyslexia diagnosis, may differ. Some parents may not want their child with reading, spelling and writing issues to be categorized as disabled. Other parents may want that classification for their child, or they may assume that the primary purpose of any assessment, whether inside or outside of the school, is to get "the diagnosis." But before your child is assessed, you should understand that this is not the case.

Varying Regulation

It's also important to understand that, like the state regulations that I mentioned in essential #13 about which professionals can diagnose dyslexia, special education codes vary from state to state. In one state, dyslexia may be officially in the code, meaning that dyslexic children are eligible for special education services, while in another state the classification system may be quite different. For example, at the time I'm writing this book, the state of New Jersey has only recently updated its special education code to include dyslexia. An assessment done by your school system, then, will take the state code into account, whereas in private testing, the assessment tends to focus more on clinical signs in making a determination.

Difference of Emphasis

With private testing, the primary focus should be on assessing the child's functioning to determine the array of strengths and weaknesses, with the fundamental underlying questions being, "Does this child have a problem or not? If so, how mild, moderate or severe is the problem?" The focus of a special education assessment is on classification, with the fundamental underlying question being, "Is this child eligible for special education services or not?"

This difference of emphasis often poses challenges for parents who are working through special education assessment, as the timetable and speed of special education assessment frequently leave parents feeling very frustrated. While things may change in the future, more often than not I hear parents saying that they started to observe issues when their child was in kindergarten, first or second grade, yet they didn't feel that the school was particularly responsive in terms of performing assessment.

From the school's vantage point, if the child is roughly within an average range and getting decent grades, then there is no need for an evaluation. The school is unlikely to do an assessment or plot a course of action until it goes through various levels of determining need. The school would track and monitor whether the child was, in fact, able to respond to the normal curriculum before making other determinations that he may need further assessment or intervention.

Often, this translates to parents as inaction and waiting to fail. And often, parents are likely to take the reins into their own hands by seeking a private consultation or assessment.

Why Get a Private Assessment?

As mentioned, parents may seek a private assessment when they observe signs of a reading struggle that has not yet been identified by the school. But even if a child is already receiving special education or extra help at school, here are some reasons why a private assessment may be a good idea.

An Assessment Is a Snapshot

Assessment provides a snapshot, a picture of the child at a moment in time. At this point in my career, I have worked with children in high school and college whom I evaluated when they were in pre-kindergarten or early elementary school. The earlier assessments offered a good reference point to see what major variables were initially identified and which of them continue to be relevant.

Assessment also provides a baseline with which to measure progress. If your child is receiving any intervention in school or through outside remediation, the testing allows you to chart progress in key areas such as decoding, word identification and instructional levels, to name a few.

Next Step Thinking

Another major purpose of testing is to guide you in taking the appropriate next steps. What type of instruction or remediation is suggested through the assessment? How frequent? What duration? Individual or small group? While testing may not give you absolute answers to these questions, you should be able to receive guidelines that answer many of them.

Obtaining a Diagnosis

Private practitioners offer commentary on diagnostic formulations once an assessment is completed. Since private practitioners aren't bound by the same regulations that may constrain school assessments, they are in a position to offer a diagnosis when the data warrants it. Such a diagnosis can be helpful in obtaining special accommodations in the classroom and possibly in receiving services through the school.

Private Testing Costs

If your child is assessed for special education services at a public school, that assessment is paid for by the school system. But if you feel the need to take action and obtain a private assessment, your family will need to consider and plan for the cost of testing.

Sometimes people think that because dyslexia is a "medical condition," insurance companies will pay for screening services. At the time I'm writing this book, however, I have not found this to be the case. Insurance companies rarely (I would almost say never) cover the assessment of learning disabilities. If you're considering a private assessment, shop around and determine a price range. Costs vary widely from region to region within the United States but testing currently ranges roughly between $1,500 and $6,000.

Understand that assessment is time-consuming. A good screening (not a computer-based one) will usually take the evaluator at least two hours of work. This includes approximately half an hour of post-assessment discussion with you, and half an hour to an hour to write a letter that sums up their findings for teachers and other professionals. More involved testing can take five or six hours, which then results in higher costs. Be sure to talk over different assessment options with the evaluator before you proceed.

The Curse of the Gray Zone

In our overview of assessment considerations, I discussed how dyslexia is often not a black and white issue, but rather occurs on a continuum. And in the previous section, I mentioned how sometimes parents can see their child struggling to read, spell and write, yet no one else seems to be especially concerned. When this happens, families often feel stuck, unable to move forward. I refer to this situation as "The Curse of the Gray Zone" or the "Zone of No Zone." At this point, I'd like to take a closer look at the Gray Zone, using a couple of examples.

Suzette, Age Nine

Suzette is a pleasant and dutiful fourth-grade child. She hands in her homework and usually exhibits a range of teacher pleasing behaviors. Whenever her parents talk to her teacher, they always hear something like, "Oh, Suzette is such a wonderful and sweet child; I wish I my whole class was like her."

While this is gratifying for her parents to hear, they can't shake their worries about Suzette. They've watched her struggle to read ever since kindergarten, and it hasn't seemed to get any easier for her. To make matters more confusing for them, in spite of the observed struggle, Suzette always gets good grades.

When her parents brought their concerns to the school's special education team to ask about an assessment, the team did not feel Suzette should be evaluated. Taking one look at her grades, one of the team members told her parents that she was "doing fine and would not be eligible for any kind of special education testing or services."

Even though from her parents' point of view Suzette is clearly having difficulty, she is not in a zone of concern according to the school's standards. Unfortunately, grades are often used as the sole yardstick in determining whether a child should be evaluated and ultimately classified for special education, even though many kids with average or good grades, like Suzette, can have undetected reading, spelling and writing problems. Also unfortunately, Suzette's pleasant disposition may actually work against her, as it might conceal just how much she is struggling. Essentially, "the squeaky wheel gets the grease" – that is, kids who get poor grades, or whose frustration is obvious or even disruptive, are more likely to get the attention they need.

Suzette came to me for a private assessment. One of her more striking test results was her difficulty with large, unfamiliar words. It's very common for fourth-grade reading assignments to include such words, and while Suzette had memorized enough words to get her through the third grade with reasonable adequacy, she hit frustration pretty quickly within her own grade level. She needed tutoring to address this weakness. However, her test scores would not qualify her for any type of special education services or even a 504 plan through her school.

Zachary, Age Seven

The case of young Zachary also illustrates the Curse of the Gray Zone. In contrast with Suzette, Zachary was tested by the special education team based on a referral from his second-grade teacher, who saw him struggling in the major areas of concern.

Once the testing was completed and a meeting was set up, Zachary's parents were hopeful that he would receive services. However, once the meeting started, they quickly realized he would not be considered eligible for services, as the vast majority of his results were found to be "within the average range."

When the parents brought Zachary's test results to me for an independent consultation, it was clear at one glance that he had a number of areas of concern, as most of his major subtest scores fell in the lower portion of the average range, between the 25th and 35th percentiles. While this range is technically "average," in most classes and in most situations, children in that zone do struggle, and they sometimes meet the overall diagnostic criteria for dyslexia.

Both Suzette's and Zachary's cases are clear examples of the Curse of the Gray Zone. As we've seen, dyslexia is not clear-cut, but children do fall roughly along a bell curve in terms of skill level. You can visualize the Gray Zone as the part of the bell curve that's left of center but not at the far left edge. Kids whose assessment scores fall in the Gray Zone may show weaknesses in the cognitive and academic functions that we've discussed in previous sections, and it's likely that they're struggling. Yet they may not be found eligible for special education or may not be diagnosable as dyslexic.

In these cases, teachers' hands may be tied in terms of taking any action. Unfortunately, there is very little that can be done to change the school's decision once it determines that a child is average. However, from my vantage point outside of a school setting, anyone on the left side of the bell curve in key areas such as word identification, reading fluency, spelling and written expression needs help, even if they are technically in the average zone. If this is the case for your child, odds are that she will not get help in school, but you can still take action. Usually this will be in the form of targeted, remedial tutoring.

Takeaway Point

Look closely at your child's testing scores, with a particular eye toward percentile ranks. Anything less than the 45th percentile in a key area of concern may represent a red flag, even if your child is technically within the average range.

Assessment: Summary and Takeaway Points

A dyslexia assessment needs to address a number of key areas that cover critical aspects of cognitive and academic functioning.

- Testing for dyslexia is a process, and there is no "dyslexia x-ray." Assessment usually consists of a battery of tests that cover key areas of language functioning.
- It's essential for an assessment to consider both the quantitative findings and the qualitative, informal information derived from the assessment. The qualitative information is clinical, meaning that an experienced clinician makes these observations as part of the assessment.
- Medical doctors, including neurologists, generally don't engage in the kind of testing that is necessary to determine dyslexia. While their commentary on the child's neurological health may be helpful, the necessary testing battery for dyslexia is different from a neurological assessment.

- Phonological processing, phonemic awareness and AWM (Active Working Memory, especially auditory sequential memory) are key predictors of dyslexia. That is, active working memory and phonemic awareness issues commonly go along with reading problems.
- Assessments serve many purposes in addition to obtaining a diagnosis. Benefits include providing a snapshot of a moment in time and guiding parents and teachers in determining the next steps to take in order to meet the child's specific needs.
- There are fundamental differences between special education assessments and assessments provided by a private clinician (psychologist). These differences are important to understand.
- Assessment guides instruction. A good assessment will help you to establish appropriate goals for any remedial instruction that your child will receive.

PART III

INTERVENTION AND INSTRUCTION

Intervention and Instructional Considerations

Once you've "cleared the brush" in terms of understanding the variables that have contributed to your child's struggling, and once you've gone through an assessment process, it's time to get down to the business of instruction and remediation. There are many instructional variables that you'll need to understand, and most of them will be covered in this part of the book.

Many dyslexia remediation approaches and programs follow the fundamental principles of the Orton-Gillingham method, which was developed in the 1940s. As I'll discuss in the next essential, these programs are also referred to as multisensory language-based instruction.

In general, these principles have held up well for decades. Many remediation programs on the market today are spin-offs of Orton-Gillingham (e.g., Wilson Language, Preventing Academic Failure, Barton, Slingerland, Lindamood-Bell and others). While I don't endorse any specific program, I will highlight the methodologies and approaches that I often recommend to my patients. From this point forward I will refer to the various programs as "Orton-based," or for the sake of variety, the "O-G methods."

Whatever specific program the parents ultimately choose, I tell them they should look for a remediation program that meets the following criteria.

As Individual as Possible

Remediation should be delivered in as individualized a format as possible. Ideally, instruction should be one-on-one, since this format allows the teacher to tailor the instruction to the child and her needs. Another advantage of one-on-one instruction is that it provides many opportunities for reinforcement, including positive comments, support and corrective feedback. Very often, this one-on-one instruction takes the form of private tutoring.

Small Group Is the Next Best

If one-on-one remediation is not possible, then the next best format is small group instruction. The challenges of a small group are primarily managerial. Children need to be well-matched based on their age and level of instructional need. Based on my experience, small instructional groups shouldn't include more than four children.

At an Appropriate Frequency

Daily instruction is ideal. But since tutoring can be expensive for many families, I often recommend twice-weekly sessions.

In terms of session duration, anything shorter than half an hour is probably just skimming the surface. Sessions that are at least half an hour long can produce good results, particularly if they take place on a daily basis. In Orton-based programs, most sessions are typically about an hour long.

Practice Rich

There should be ample opportunity for reading practice. Children move from using controlled text (i.e., text where the reading demands are limited to the skill being taught) to practicing with less-controlled text (i.e., text that includes regular and irregular words with a variety of different syllable types).

Skill Focused

Compared to more general reading instruction, which is literature-based and story-focused, dyslexia remediation follows very clear, established, targeted instructional methods. Probably the most important aspect of good remediation, then, is that it is as laser-focused as possible. Make sure that your child's instructor is clear on the goal of the remediation and on the goals and targets of the instruction. If the instructional remediation is scattershot in its approach, it will probably not be that effective.

Not Rushed

Individual skills are taught one at a time until they are mastered and sufficiently internalized. Explicit and direct instruction should lead to measurable progress. Even though some kids who have lagged behind in fundamental decoding skills may make quick initial progress, time is still needed for those skills to really take hold.

Multisensory Methodologies – The Primary Ingredients

There are many remedial treatments for dyslexia that are built on Orton-Gillingham principles and follow those established methodologies. Collectively, these programs are also referred to as multisensory language-based instruction. While the various programs have their differences, they share many similarities.

Some common multisensory methodologies include:

- Barton Reading & Spelling System
- Lindamood-Bell (LIPS)
- Project Assist
- Project Read
- Orton-Gillingham
- Reading Horizons
- S.P.I.R.E
- Wilson Reading System

As you start to investigate these methods and why they work, there are a few points to keep in mind. To identify these

points, let's break down the core principles of the multisensory
remedial methodologies.

Reading Is a Skill and Must Be Directly Taught and Practiced

This is the driving principle behind multisensory language-based instruction, and it may seem obvious to many
people. However, there has been an ongoing debate about this
point over the decades, and it's been at the heart of the great
"reading wars" that have taken place within modern educational systems.

There is an opposing perspective, in which reading is a
natural process that just emerges. Proponents of this view
tend to teach reading using what I refer to as the "osmosis"
approach. The underlying philosophy here is that when children are allowed to interact along the buffet table of literature, their skills will unfold naturally and will blossom and
develop. Teachers function as guides and facilitators, but
reading skills develop organically through osmosis and exposure. Children learn incidentally how to combine sounds
and words. This approach has been the primary vehicle for
teaching reading for decades. It has gone through different it-
erations. For a long time it was known as the "whole language
approach" and it took hold across the country and in university education departments. The major problem with this
approach is that it works fine for about 60 percent of the population, but simply does not work for the rest of the children
who are struggling. For this group, the osmosis approach that
is based on exposure to literature and worksheets does not
work for many reasons.

In my work with children and parents, I always emphasize that reading is a skill that can be subdivided into component skills, much like sports or music. For example, in tennis there are the skills of hitting forehand and of hitting backhand. While there are similarities between forehand and backhand, there are also differences. Some lucky individuals by observation and osmosis can hit a ball fairly well in both ways without any direct instruction, but many more people will need to be taught these skills directly, and they'll need to practice over time to internalize them.

When it comes to music, I've taken guitar lessons over the years and vividly remember how difficult it is to learn to move between one chord and another. There is the clumsy period of time when the chord switches are slow and quite awkward. I had to practice the switches hundreds, if not thousands of times before they became second nature.

In my observation, children who are struggling to read need similar, ongoing practice for a sufficient period of time to internalize fundamental reading skills. Within a program such as the Orton-based methods, children first practice individual sounds and letters. This is somewhat analogous to practicing notes on the piano. From there, sounds are put into words that are presented in isolation (reminiscent of chords). Once these words are internalized and mastered, the child reads them in a more extended text, much like chords and notes appear in a full piece of music. In both music and reading, guided instruction and ongoing practice are essential to help develop fluency and mastery.

Some years ago, I was gratified to see a *New York Times* article focusing on a specialized school, The Windward School. The article references a Ms. Bertin, the director at the time:

Ms. Bertin likens the school (The Windward School) to a conservatory where aspiring musicians practice scales and play exercises to prepare themselves for the masterworks they one day hope to play. Ms. Bertin says the nation's sense of having a reading crisis will only deepen until school systems and colleges of education adopt a structured approach that reaches the 4 in 10 American children who have trouble learning to read.

"Windward is not the answer," Ms. Bertin said. "The answer is to change the way we teach teachers to teach reading." (*New York Times*, 2002, "How Learning to Read a Book Is Like Learning to Play the Piano")

Some children can pick up a guitar and interact with the instrument, figuring out finger placements and chords, seemingly learning those skills by osmosis. For most children, this isn't the case. It's the same way with reading. There are some children who can interact with the osmosis-buffet table and become functional readers with the necessary skills. Others – and this is the group that we are concerned with – need direct instruction and guided practice. They must learn to play the notes, play the chords, then put them together into music.

Direct (Explicit) vs. Incidental

I just mentioned in my discussion of the osmosis approach that word and sound combination skills are learned incidentally, that is, primarily through reading stories and answering questions. This type of reading instruction has been around for years, and while it may work for kids who aren't struggling with decoding and reading fluency, it's a poor instructional match for children with dyslexia. The multisensory methodologies work for dyslexic kids because they don't rely on incidental learning. Rather, the skills are directly taught, and they are broken down into their components one subskill at a time. This direct instruction is a hallmark of the O-G multisensory methodologies.

Another feature of direct instruction is that it incorporates straightforward and immediate feedback. For example, a child in an individualized remediation session probably receives thirty to fifty direct feedback statements from her instructor over the course of a one-hour lesson. Through these statements, the instructor corrects the child if she makes a mistake or provides positive reinforcement when she does a task correctly. In a classroom lesson, on the other hand, it's almost impossible for any one child to receive more than a couple of direct comments to reinforce or guide him in his reading. Immediate feedback is a major component of direct instruction and one of the most valuable aspects of multisensory instruction.

Simultaneous Multisensory

We've been using the word *multisensory,* and this might be making you think of an overwhelming sensory experience. However, in the context of Orton-based methods, *simultaneous multisensory* just means that many senses are engaged at the same time while the child is being instructed. In this case, that's a good thing. Far too often, children are instructed via worksheets and reading materials that aren't particularly stimulating. Think about it: when a child is given a worksheet, they're really only using one sense – the visual. With multisensory instruction, the child may be listening, visualizing, and touching letters or felt cubes at the same time. Often there is movement involved too, as a child is encouraged to move letters and letter groupings around or stand at a white board and engage with colored markers.

Sequential and Systematic

Another key component of the Orton-based or multisensory methods is their sequential nature. The methods follow a clear sequence. One skill leads to the next. You only move forward when the skill has been clearly mastered.

Not only is there a clear sequence in the skills that are taught, but each lesson is also highly sequential. Once the child has been taught a few times with the multisensory methods, he comes to know each activity of the lesson quite well. They follow a very consistent routine that the child comes to rely upon during the course of instruction.

Highly Individualized

As I mentioned in the overview, a good remediation strategy will either be individualized or involve a very small group of no more than three or four kids. The Orton-based methodologies fit this bill exactly, and the individualized nature allows for proper pacing and maximizes the amount of feedback your child will receive. Too often children are moved through an instructional program too quickly before the skills have been fully consolidated, but the multisensory methods avoid rushing the child.

The Decoding Hurdle

Having assessed thousands of kids over the course of my professional career, I believe that there is a fundamental learning task of early childhood that can be one of the most essential hurdles for a child to get over – I call it the decoding hurdle.

Decoding, as you may remember, is the ability to decipher words automatically and efficiently. Dyslexics are fundamentally poor at decoding. As noted in the section on the Matthew Effects, when a child doesn't conquer the decoding hurdle, a type of bottleneck forms, which can affect many aspects of a child's learning and school performance.

For a child on the smooth road, this hurdle is not too big of a deal. With normal interactions and typical instruction, they get over it. Children with dyslexia, meanwhile, don't get over this hurdle easily, and it affects their self-esteem deeply. Reverberations of this struggle can last well into adulthood.

Take Frank, a forty-five-year-old father of a child who was brought in to see me for a consultation. As Frank explained the concerns he had with his own child, he recounted what life was like for him some years back:

People don't understand how hard it was. I detested reading because of the phonics, the decoding, as you call it. I couldn't figure out words like other children could, and it scarred me throughout elementary school and then later into middle and high school. Even though I became successful at running a business, I've always been embarrassed by the fact that reading (and spelling and writing) was problematic. Sure, I found ways around it. My wife has been an enormous help, but I still feel the deep wounds, and I try to avoid that for my child. I understand there's a hurdle that she has to overcome, but I see how hard it is for her.

Early in a child's life, we typically focus on the more physical and social developmental tasks like walking, talking and toilet training. I think people rarely understand the importance of getting over the decoding hurdle. From my perspective, decoding is just as real and meaningful as any physical development, since it deeply affects learning, which is the main task of childhood. If a child doesn't get over this hurdle, their learning progress slows down, they fall behind their peers, and all sorts of psychological fallout occurs, such as feelings of anxiety, low self-worth and depression.

When you understand the decoding hurdle for what it is, then you're better prepared to take effective, early action. Think about it this way: when children in preschool struggle with speech, we don't hesitate. We get them help in the form of a speech and language therapist. The same should be true with decoding. While not all children who are slow in getting over this hurdle turn out to be dyslexic, as some are true "late bloomers," the fact is that a significant number of them are dyslexic, and the struggle never really goes away.

Takeaway Point

We can save ourselves a great deal of time, aggravation and expense if we call the decoding hurdle out for what it is – and recognize that it represents a fundamental, if not *the* fundamental task of early childhood.

The Orton-Gillingham Programs Can't Be Rushed

One of the most important things to keep in mind when it comes to the Orton-based programs is that they typically take a long time and cannot be rushed. The length of time your child will need depends on a number of factors. These include age, developmental level when the program starts, the child's level of cognitive functioning and the severity of the reading problem. Additionally, the amount of remediation that the child will receive is a major determinant of the program's ultimate pace.

Let's look at a few of those variables.

Child's Age

As a general rule, the younger the child is when the program starts, the quicker the pace of the remedial progress. This is because younger children seem to have fewer points of resistance and fewer layers of negative experience to work through, and they are generally more open to instruction. There are a few more potential obstacles for older children. The O-G methods are very basic in terms of the skills being developed, and older children sometimes erroneously think of the program as "babyish." This may lead to some level of increased resistance, particularly if the program is being offered outside of school in a tutorial format. Many older children are often shut-down learners, and this resistance also slows down the rate of progress.

Level of Cognitive Functioning

For the sake of both the kids and the parents, it's important for parents to be realistic about their child's level of cognitive functioning. If a child's cognitive levels are significantly below average (e.g., below the 10th percentile), as determined by a test such as the WISC-V, then parents and teachers will need to adjust their expectations for progress. This certainly doesn't mean that you can't expect any improvement at all, but as a parent, it's important to have a reasonable, realistic sense of what your child is capable of if given sufficient attention. It's often helpful to talk with the psychologist who did her testing, as well as with her teacher or tutor, about what you may realistically expect.

Frequency and Intensity of Remediation

There is tremendous variation in the intensity of remediation among the children and families that I see. Some children get twenty minutes of instruction in each of their twice-weekly group sessions, others have an hour of private instruction every day, and I've seen every possibility in between. The guiding principle here should be that your child's level of skill deficiency or severity should guide the intensity of the instruction.

Frequency and intensity will both affect the pace of progress under the O-G methods, but understand that even under the most ideal circumstances, the program will not be a quick fix. Ideally, a child would receive remediation on an individual basis for about an hour or so each day, but at the minimum, I would encourage you to seek at least two one-hour sessions per week.

"Under-the-Hood" Variables

As part of my car analogy that I've come back to at times throughout this book, I've referred to the under-the-hood variables that affect the efficiency of reading performance. Most of these variables fall under the category of phonological processes, such as phonemic awareness, phonological segmentation, rhyming, active working memory and rapid naming ability.

Some of the more common tests used to assess these variables are the CTOPP-2 and the RAN-2. Have your evaluator review these to determine whether your child was mildly below average or more deficient in the factors assessed. The more deficient the phonological processes, the slower the rate of progress you will need to expect.

Student/Teacher Connection

Another factor in the rate of progress is inherent in the nature of the Orton-based approaches, and it's an issue that isn't discussed enough in teacher training or with parents. This is the need for emotional engagement between the teacher and the child. Between the teacher/learning therapist and the child, there's an intangible interaction that can, and should, give the child a great deal of "emotional fuel" (motivation).

This might sound heretical for me to say, but I've seen Orton-based methods delivered letter-perfectly and yet they have little impact on the child, even when the child is in desperate need of remediation. It is my hypothesis that this occurs when the delivery is dry and unenthused, resulting in no igniting of emotion or overcoming of discouragement. The skill work contained in a typical O-G lesson can be dry enough, but if the work is coupled with a teacher who is not lively, engaged and engaging, then the result will be disconnected kids with bored faces. The motivation will be low and the progress slow. The sense of insecurity and discouragement experienced by dyslexic kids is pervasive enough already, and if they sense that they are not understood or supported, even a textbook O-G lesson will not click for them.

Here's an example of what that might look like.

Harry, Age Nine

Harry leaves his classroom three times a week to take part in a small group Orton-based program. Harry's teacher in that small group, Mrs. Finch, believes that teaching phonics (or decoding) requires a "drill and kill" approach, so she's never quite embraced the need to teach sounds and isolated words as required in the Orton-based programs. She prefers the approaches that emphasize comprehension and higher order thinking. When the district changed their policy, however, Mrs. Finch was required to take advanced training to address the needs of dyslexic children. She was not overly thrilled about this. "Special groups for dyslexic children," Mrs. Finch thought, "yet another new thing that the school is throwing onto our plates. I'm not sure I'm equipped to handle this, but I have no choice but to comply." Mrs. Finch's lack of enthusiasm for, or understanding of, the Orton-based methods and their underlying rationale results in technically correct lessons delivered in a dull, flat monotone style.

Meanwhile, Harry complains bitterly about his small group each night to his parents. He hates going to the resource room. The lessons are stupid, babyish and meaningless, and he wants his parents to get him out of there. Clearly, because of the way the program is being delivered, Harry's progress will be slow.

No Mastery Without Practice

I've mentioned the Smooth Road kids and how the process of learning to read works for them: skills building on top of skills in a cumulative fashion, a sense of personal gratification that leads to a positive snowball effect and a continual resupplying of the emotional fuel in their tank. These children don't need much intentional practice of specific skills in order to master a new task. But that's not the case with dyslexic kids. Skills are not acquired naturally or effortlessly, and their need for repeated practice over time is far greater.

Often, when I see children who are receiving tutoring outside of school and still not mastering reading skills, this sustained repetition over time is the missing ingredient. Many parents may decide that the Orton-based methods are too time-consuming or too expensive and pull the child out of remediation before they've done enough sustained practice.

I've also seen the Orton-based methods fail because the parents not only wanted the whole process to take less time, but wanted to move through each stage more quickly. It can be tempting for both the child and the parent to rush the process, starting the next skill or substep before the current one is totally solid. But if a child is moved along too quickly, problems will often arise later.

If your child is receiving Orton-based remediation or special education in a school setting, this essential – be patient, don't rush – is also necessary for the school staff to understand. Teachers and learning therapists all need to understand your child's goals fully so that everyone working with him can allow the time for sufficient practice and mastery of each skill.

Takeaway Point

The seemingly slow pace of progress is understandably frustrating, but it helps to know about the many variables contributing to the pace. Understanding these variables will help you be aware of how your child is responding to the interventions that are in place, and it may also help you to be patient with the lengthy process and celebrate his successes. Remember that while the slow and steady pace required by the Orton-based methods may be exasperating, it may be worth it in the end.

Improvement Does Not Always Mean Immediate Fluency

I've observed the progress of thousands of kids over the years, and I've watched them receive excellent decoding-emphasis instruction using what I know to be the best methodologies, from enthusiastic, warm, supportive, knowledgeable teachers. Invariably, children make progress in decoding when the Orton-based methods are used, and the child's skill development increases along with their confidence.

However, one area that remains extraordinarily difficult to develop is reading fluency. Reading fluency and improved decoding are, unfortunately, not synonymous.

Reading fluency is one of the five major components of reading, as identified in a landmark 2000 research report from the National Reading Panel. (The other components are phonemic awareness, phonics, vocabulary and comprehension.) Virtually all dyslexic children have some degree of difficulty with reading fluency.

Practice, Practice, Practice

There is one overriding way to develop fluency, and after the last essential, it may sound familiar – practice, practice, practice. There is no getting around it. This practice can be done in two ways: informally or with more formal programs that specifically target reading fluency.

The informal approach is one you can do with books and other reading material you already have at home. Find something that you know is on your child's independent reading level (that is, the level where he finds the material to be relatively easy). You can give him material that is slightly above the easy level, but you don't want to go too far beyond that point.

Have him read out loud at that independent level for about ten minutes a night. Make it fun and lively. Put a big green check on a calendar after he has done ten minutes of reading aloud. After a bunch of checks have accumulated, go out and celebrate with a small reward (like an ice cream sundae or toy from the dollar store). The point of this routine is that when a child is working on reading fluency, practice is key. This is especially the case for a dyslexic child, as compared to a Smooth Road child who doesn't have a reading disability.

The more formal approaches to fluency follow a similar strategy, only instead of picking the reading material from your child's bookshelf, you would buy a specially made workbook or series of books. These programs arrange reading material appropriately, starting at the easiest levels and increasing to the more difficult. The child reads the same stories out loud until they are fully mastered, then he reads the next story in the sequence.

I've had the opportunity to work with a parent who is also an Orton-based instructor, and she has shared some of her strategies for developing fluency:

> You can offer your child several options to encourage practice. I used to have my son choose a book that his peers were reading but that he could not access. Once he read out loud for ten to twenty minutes from a book at his level, I would read his book of choice for the same amount of time or more, depending on how quickly he read for us. As he got older, he used audiobooks to accomplish the same task. Hearing a good reader is also helpful for the struggling reader.
>
> Since electronic devices are so common today, I've had students who just record themselves and play it for the tutor or parent. You can also send it in an audio file to the tutor or parent. This is an excellent way for the tutor to hear how the student's independent reading is progressing.

As with all the other aspects of dyslexia remediation, resist any urge to rush through the development of fluency. Like the O-G methods, it's a slow process, but with good, focused and targeted approaches, your child can make progress.

Takeaway Point

Keep it light and keep it fun. Celebrate small successes.

Make Things Visual

When my daughter was studying vocabulary for the SATs, she used an interesting approach that helped her recall the words more effectively. She added a visual anchor to each of the words to help her to picture the word's definition. For example, one of the vocabulary words was "supine," and on the index card for that word she had a little stick figure picture of a pig lying on its back. All these years later I can still remember the picture, which also helps me recall the definition of the word.

While all children can benefit from making things visual, dyslexic children in particular need this kind of approach, as it serves to accomplish a number of things.

First off, visuals make the material more multisensory. Words become images or other graphic representations. Additionally, a visual approach puts the child in a more active role when they're reading or studying – activities that so many kids approach passively.

I encourage visual thinking not just because it helps kids recall vocabulary words or key terms, but as a way of increasing reading comprehension skills and managing mathematical word problems. For instance, if kids understand that a word problem is a form of a story that has a beginning, middle and end, then they can represent this story visually. I have kids divide a page into four sections or quadrants. The upper left quadrant represents the beginning of the story, the second and third quadrants are the events in the middle, and the last quadrant represents the resolution. While it's possible that some word problems might not lend themselves to this approach, I've found the vast majority do.

There were children skating on a pond.	One child went to a section where they were told not go.

The ice started to break apart and the child panicked. A dog close by started to bark loudly, alerting parents.	Parents were able to rescue the child before he slipped through the ice.

Drawing: Nathan Bond

This four-quadrant method also works nicely with chapter-book reading. When your child starts reading a chapter book, buy a sketchbook, and guide and encourage her to map out in picture form what happens in each chapter. This helps kids to summarize and engage more actively with the material.

When using a visual approach that involves drawing, teachers, tutors, and parents should try to dissuade kids from getting too hung up on the quality of their pictures, as some children will protest that they lack artistic skills or are "so bad at drawing." Remind them that even basic stick figures work nicely with this approach.

In addition to drawing, children can also be taught and encouraged to use mind-mapping applications. Software programs and apps like Inspiration use visual mapping in the form of shapes, images, lines, arrows and other visual elements to engage the user in creating a graphic representation of their thoughts and ideas. Most kids find that mind mapping is fun and helps with recall and planning. (For more information on mind mapping, see the Visual Leap website.)

As we've seen in many of the examples in this book, dyslexics on average perform better with spatial and nonverbal tasks such as Legos or on assessments such as Block Design and Matrix Reasoning. If your child has these strengths, capitalize on them by training her to make everything visual when she reads and studies. The earlier children figure out a process that works for them and start using it, the better. I know many college students who automatically use visual studying and reading methods they learned when they were younger, with significant effects on their grades and overall academic performance.

One reason I believe these visual approaches work so well is that they put the child more in charge of his own learning.

So many of the kids that I've seen over the years are passive learners. There is little notetaking while reading and few attempts to adapt or optimize their learning style. But when a child or adult takes responsibility for his learning, it's likely to be a more emotionally satisfying experience, which leads to better engagement with the material and the learning process.

One final point about these visual learning approaches: they don't happen automatically, and they're usually developed and shown to the child by a good tutor who can open the child's mind to new methods and ways of reading and studying. Children will usually give their parents a fair amount of pushback if parents try to encourage these approaches, but they'll rarely give a tutor "stuff" in the form of resistance.

Takeaway Point

Every chance you can, make it visual – and enlist your child's tutor, teacher or learning specialist to help.

Maintain a Two-Column Mindset

Parents usually want guidance in helping their child overcome her difficulties, and they also often want to rush into things and hurry it along. But as we've discussed, hurrying rarely helps.

Fortunately, there's a way you can think about your child's dyslexia that will help you reduce the urge to rush and will manage any feelings of helplessness on her behalf. When I review assessment findings with parents, I frequently find myself in front of the white board mapping out different ideas and concepts. One of my favorite things to show parents is the notion of a two-column mindset when thinking about what can be done with their dyslexic child.

The two columns are:

Interventions	Accommodations (or Ways Around the Problem)

I call this a *mindset* rather than just a chart because I see these two columns as the things you should start thinking about once you understand the nature of your child's learning disability. These two categories, interventions and accommodations, should always be in the back of your mind – and occasionally brought to the foreground – as she progresses in school.

Interventions are things that are done to or with the child in order to directly address her reading problem. For example, Orton-based remediation would be an intervention, as would any other reading or instructional method. Other therapies, such as occupational therapy or speech and language therapy, would also be in the intervention column, as would any type of counseling, like Cognitive Behavioral Therapy (CBT). If your child is on any medication, such as Adderall or Concerta, then these medications are also interventions.

Mind you, I'm not saying that all dyslexic children need all of these interventions. Each child needs to be considered on an individual basis. For some kids, the only intervention, and the only item in that left-hand column of the chart above, will be tutoring, while another child may be getting half a dozen therapies.

The same goes for the right-hand side of the chart, the "accommodations" column. To fill out the "accommodations" column, write down anything that you, your child's teacher, school, or tutor may be doing to help him around the problem. Keep in mind that some of these may be done informally and may not be drawn up in a 504 plan or an IEP. You may have started many of these accommodations a long time ago, before your child even started remediation.

Examples of accommodations include:

- Previewing words with your child prior to reading.
- Reading material that you know will be difficult out loud to your child.
- Using Assistive Technology (AT) and having chapter books read aloud on something like Learning Ally.
- In the classroom, making sure directions are repeated and your child receives help getting oriented to the task.
- Providing extra time if that is helpful.
- Offering notetaking assistance.
- Allowing children to take photos of notes rather than copying notes by hand.
- Not penalizing for spelling.

In my experience, parents tend to over-focus on the left-hand column, the interventions, often forgetting how important it is to implement and maintain accommodations. I've observed that as the child gets older (i.e., twelve years and up), it becomes increasingly necessary to keep accommodations front and center. Accommodations and workarounds help empower your child to take increasingly greater responsibility for his own learning, given his learning style and needs.

One example of this is a boy named Mitchell, who had severe learning disabilities and whom I worked with for many years. As Mitchell entered high school, he increasingly embraced a range of AT tools that helped him feel that he was taking charge of his learning in ways that he otherwise couldn't.

As Mitchell explained to me, "At the end of class I wait for everyone to go out and then I take out my phone and take a photo of anything on the board. For any extensive reading, I see if it's on Learning Ally, and if it's not, then I have the material scanned and it's read to me through Kurzweill 3000. I also am getting better at using Dragon Naturally Speaking to dictate my ideas for writing. Nothing's perfect, but it certainly is a lot better than not using it."

Takeaway Point

Always maintain a two-column mindset when your child has been diagnosed with a learning disability such as dyslexia. As she gets older, the accommodations on the right side of the chart play an increasing role in her academic performance and everyday life.

Dyslexia into Adulthood

I evaluate many students who are starting high school or college, and I even see adults who are either already in the workforce or looking for employment. Their age and level of development call for different considerations than I would apply to younger children.

First, as I've stated previously, the Orton-based programs are time-consuming. Given the typical busy schedule of a high school or college student, twice-weekly Orton-based tutoring would be very challenging. For this reason, then, it's even more important to create accommodations or workarounds, as I called them in the previous essential, to help the dyslexic teenager or adult function in school or the workplace.

I would like to use an example of a college student I tested recently to illustrate the most important considerations for older students and adults.

Ryan, Age Twenty-One

Ryan came to me because he suspected that he had dyslexia, even though he'd never been evaluated. He spoke eloquently about the pervasive sense of embarrassment he experienced while he was in middle and high school. Hiding in the shadows of the classroom, Ryan desperately tried to avoid being shamed in front of his fellow students. Dreading being called upon to read in class, he remembered a teacher banning him from reading out loud.

My testing revealed that Ryan was clearly dyslexic. He struggled with oral reading fluency: his reading was laborious and effortful, and he performed within a sixth-grade range. Ryan also struggled greatly with low frequency multisyllabic words, and his spelling and writing were quite problematic.

I told Ryan that his suspicions had been confirmed, and then we went on to discuss actions and future direction. While Ryan may want to work on his decoding and fluency, it could take quite some time to see any improvement, even if he could come in for tutoring/learning therapy twice a week. Realistically, it's unlikely that Ryan has the time for that kind of commitment, and I question whether it would ultimately be worth his while.

As an adult, Ryan should be thinking about how he can work around the dyslexia to meet his goals. As I mentioned in the previous essential, I've known students who use AT and receive special accommodations in the classroom and during tests. In fact, I know some people who have gone to graduate school reading and writing entirely through alternative means.

"Think about it this way," I told Ryan. "What if you had a severe visual impairment and were virtually, if not totally blind. What would you do? You'd be thinking of ways to work around the impairment. You'd be looking for appropriate accommodations and technology, so you could get in the game."

I encouraged Ryan to advocate for himself: he should go to the office of student services, get a 504 plan in place, then explore the different technologies.

After I evaluated Ryan, we discussed some accommodations that might help him succeed in college. Your teenager or adult child might find some of these solutions helpful, whether she is newly diagnosed with dyslexia or just making a transition to a new school setting.

Possible Accommodations for Dyslexia

The following were the accommodations that actually appeared in Ryan's assessment report:

- If Ryan is in an academic setting, he needs to have a 504 plan in place. He will need a range of reasonable accommodations that his school or university can develop in consultation with him. I offered the following as guidelines for developing his 504 plan:
    - Ryan should be given a time extension (double time or more) when needed for classroom and standardized tests. He works very slowly and needs time to process information and will require a time extension for virtually all tests. He should also be given the opportunity to take exams in a distraction-free environment if he feels the need to do so.
    - Test modifications, with attention to font sizing, spacing and the amount of material on the page, would be helpful. Ryan could offer feedback as to whether he finds the given material overwhelming or not and whether material would need to be modified.

- Whenever possible, test items should be presented in a multiple-choice format. Ryan will find open-ended writing tests to be quite challenging and frustrating.
- If Ryan does not do well on a test, he should be given the option of taking a retest of the material at a later date.
- Ryan will need assistance with notetaking. It may be helpful for him to have access to notes or Power-Point slides prior to a lecture or class.
- Since Ryan has had difficulty with oral reading/reading fluency, teachers should not have him read out loud in class unless he volunteers. To avoid any potential embarrassment on his part relative to his spelling and writing, his classmates should not be put in a position to edit his written work.
- It would be helpful if teachers would preview work-sheets, tests, and assignments with Ryan before he starts an activity. In particular, teachers should make sure that he is able to read most of the complex words on the page.
- To the extent that it's appropriate, Ryan should be given the opportunity to respond to essay questions orally instead of in a written essay format. He has great difficulty with written expression, so he may not be able to sufficiently convey his understanding of the subject matter.
- Since writing and copying are very inefficient for Ryan, realistic expectations should be established relative to his copying from the board, as he may be unable to keep up with the other students in this

regard. Whenever possible and appropriate, teachers should provide him with supplementary written notes.

- Since he struggles with written expression, Ryan should not be penalized for spelling errors, especially when he is not in a position to utilize any type of spell check. This accommodation should particularly apply to any open-ended writing tasks.
- Ryan should be provided with opportunities to utilize graphic organizers (such as Inspiration) whenever possible to help him organize ideas prior to writing. He would need assistance in using such a program.
- In order to assist Ryan with notetaking, he should be allowed to use any of the following in the classroom:
  ○ Video and/or audio recording devices
  ○ Smart Pen (or other mobile device) to assist with notetaking
  ○ Laptop, tablet, or iPad to assist in independent notetaking
- Ryan should be given these options during a test:
  ○ The use of a reader (person or assistive technology)
  ○ The use of a calculator

- In addition to his 504 plan and the accommodations above, Ryan may also benefit from executive function coaching, which would help him to take more responsibility for his own learning, given his learning style. Executive function coaching is designed to help participants establish specific goals, practice internalizing these goals over time, and develop self-awareness. In Ryan's case, once these different skills are practiced and internalized, they will become part of his academic repertoire and, later, part of his professional skillset.

- My evaluation of Ryan suggests that he can respond better when material is reinforced through visual means. Fortunately, visual reinforcement is a skill that can be practiced and reviewed in tutoring/coaching. For example, if he associates visual pictures with the vocabulary words he needs to memorize, this opens up more multisensory means of processing information and therefore helps him remember the vocabulary terms. Utilizing different visual mapping strategies would also help him to process information. As is the case with executive function skills, it will take time for these visual reinforcement skills to become an automatic part of his repertoire.

Since Ryan is a student, my recommendations for him are tailored to a university setting. However, he'll also be able to use many of these strategies and tools in the workplace. Dyslexic adults in many different professions can use graphic organizers, AT tools, and visual reinforcement techniques, and many find additional workarounds that help them meet their job and career goals.

Takeaway Point

While targeted remediation may be helpful, and the two-column mindset should still apply, be aware that older teenagers or adults will usually get more mileage out of targeted accommodation or other workaround strategies. As your child enters a new educational environment or moves from school to the workplace, she'll need to advocate for herself and be patient with herself as she learns how to adopt new strategies and adapt the ones she has already learned. As the parent of an adult child, you may not be able to fight her battles for her, but you can be there with encouragement and support.

The Trajectory of the Positive

In this last of our twenty-five essentials, I'd like to emphasize what I call the "trajectory of the positive." That is, for the vast majority of kids that I have seen over the years, their overall trajectory, the unfolding of their life's ultimate direction, has been largely positive. I hope this will be heartening news.

When parents first contact me, though, they're often feeling less than hopeful. Usually they're in the middle of a storm, a challenge that has become overwhelming. At those times, the parent typically sees that their child is also overwhelmed by what the school is asking him to do, and the kid is shut-down or feeling frustrated.

Some time ago I heard Dr. Sally Shaywitz, author of *Overcoming Dyslexia*, talk about the child being surrounded by a "sea of strengths," a concept that has stayed with me. I've used this idea often in talking to parents, and I think it's applicable to most families' situations.

Try asking yourself: What are my child's small, medium and large strengths? Then use your answers to create a map or some other kind of visualization.

As an example, I've mapped the sea of strengths of one boy whom I saw recently:

Ultimately, building on the child's personal strengths and recognizing the many strengths that surround him helps to change his trajectory for the better over time. When kids have a supportive team – caring parents, good tutors, understanding teachers – the trajectory is usually quite good, even if the child is struggling through the storm right now.

Of course, the opposite is also true, in the sense that destructive family systems, insensitive teachers, etc., will make it harder for a child to develop a positive trajectory. In my experience, though, this phenomenon is rarer.

Takeaway Point

The more your child is surrounded by a sea of strengths, the better his journey will be, and the easier it will be for him to achieve a positive trajectory. Develop an awareness, and help him to develop an awareness, of all the strengths around him.

In Conclusion

I know we've covered our twenty-five essentials, but as I come to the end of this book, I feel a need to leave you with a few "Selznickian Truths," for what they're worth. In no particular order, here they are:

- 90 percent of all significant academic problems are connected to reading, spelling and writing issues that show up in mild, moderate or severe packages.
- Most kids fall in the mild to moderate zone. Kids who fall in the red zone of severe dyslexia, which I refer to as the "Dyslexic Hall of Fame," are much rarer.
- You need to focus on the decoding hurdle to try to help your child over it. The earlier, the better.
- If your child can't get over the decoding hurdle, don't give up, but be realistic.
- Large words are kryptonite to dyslexic children. These words start showing up a lot in the fourth grade.
- Reading, spelling and writing are skills that can ultimately be improved. Some people are wired to learn these skills easily – others are not.

- In the early years, about half of all children will learn to read regardless of what teaching method is used. They progress no matter what. It's the other half who need instruction delivered at a slower pace and broken down into little bitty bites for them to digest better.
- Expanding on the above point, about half of all children will also need instruction delivered more explicitly and directly than the popular "osmosis methods" allow.
- A lot of school work is busy work. Homework is largely pointless, but it does teach kids the important value of managing your time and your stuff. Homework is more about executive function development than anything else.
- Most worksheets are dreadful for all kids, but they're especially dreadful for struggling kids.
- Open-ended writing is the worst, most challenging and most unfair activity for dyslexic children. It is beyond kryptonite.
- School districts are not equipped to readily understand or manage the problems of dyslexic children. At some point or multiple points in your child's education, you will need to advocate for her and possibly even take things into your own hands.
- Kids don't have to be classified or diagnosed as learning disabled to benefit from support and practical help. Struggling is struggling.
- The Full Scale IQ tells us very little about the child, yet the WISC-V (the gold standard of IQ tests) can be very helpful. It's the entire profile that matters much more than the FSIQ.
- Even kids with low IQ scores deserve and need help. They should not be held hostage by their IQ.

- I feel so strongly about the above point that I'm going to repeat it: if the kid is struggling, get him help.
- For children with learning disabilities, particularly dyslexia, please stop dwelling on grades or the SATs. Water finds its own level; so do children, ultimately. You may be able to get your child into a school like Georgetown or some other top tier college, but if she won't be comfortable doing sustained work at that level, is that really the best thing for her?
- Above all, remember, "This too shall pass." Kids find their way. Their many strengths take them there.

RESOURCES

Warning Signs of Dyslexia

(This list is copyrighted by Susan M. Barton, the founder of Bright Solutions for Dyslexia, www.BrightSolutions.US. It is reprinted here with prior written permission from Susan Barton.)

In Preschool

- delayed speech
- mixing up the sounds and syllables in long words
- chronic ear infections
- stuttering
- constant confusion of left versus right
- late establishing a dominant hand
- difficulty learning to tie shoes
- trouble memorizing their address, phone number or the alphabet
- can't create words that rhyme
- a close relative with dyslexia

In Elementary School

- dysgraphia (slow, non-automatic handwriting that is difficult to read)
- letter or number reversals continuing past the end of first grade

- extreme difficulty learning cursive
- slow, choppy, inaccurate reading:
    - guesses based on shape or context
    - skips or misreads prepositions (as, to, of)
    - ignores suffixes
    - can't sound out unknown words
- terrible spelling
- often can't remember sight words (they, work, does) or homonyms (their, they're and there)
- difficulty telling time with a clock with hands
- trouble with math (memorizing multiplication tables; memorizing a sequence of steps; directionality)
- when speaking, difficulty finding the correct words (lots of "whatyamacallits" and "thingies")
- common sayings coming out slightly twisted
- extremely messy bedroom, backpack and desk
- dreads going to school - complains of stomachaches or headaches; may have nightmares about school

In High School
All of the above symptoms plus:

- limited vocabulary, extremely poor written expression (large discrepancy between verbal skills and written composition)
- unable to master a foreign language
- difficulty reading printed music
- may drop out of high school

In Adults
- slow reader
- may have to read a page two or three times to understand it

- terrible speller
- difficulty putting thoughts onto paper—dreads writing memos or letters
- still has difficulty with right versus left
- often gets lost, even in a familiar city
- sometimes confuses *b* and *d*, especially when tired or sick

Stages of Reading Development and Instructional Guidelines

The following chart is intended to be used as a guideline. The column to the left describes the typical skills developed within a given stage. It is important to emphasize that these are approximate guidelines and there is no strict demarcation from one stage to another. As a general rule, it is better to stay in a stage longer than to move a child forward prematurely. The stages of reading development are applicable to all children, not just those identified as dyslexic. The stages provide a type of roadmap to guide instruction and next-step thinking.

	INSTRUCTIONAL GOALS	COMMON PROGRAMS
Stage 0 Typically corresponds from preschool though end of kindergarten. Formal reading skills have not been obtained in this stage.	Identify upper- & lower-case letters by name. Identify sounds that are associated with the letters. Introduce small numbers of sight words once letters are known.	Wilson Fundations, Neuhaus, Spire, Barton, Reading Horizons

	INSTRUCTIONAL GOALS	COMMON PROGRAMS
Early Stage One Typically corresponds to the first half of first grade. Introducing limited high frequency (sight words). Basic decoding. Typically, words are simplistic and mono-syllabic.	Solidify sight words. Target words with simple c-v-c patterns such as (e.g., met, rib, mob, tin). Spelling of sight words mentioned above, as well as the c-v-c word patterns. Writing of simple sentences including words above.	Any of the common multisensory programs mentioned earlier are appropriate. Common sight word lists available.
Later Stage One Typically corresponds to the second half of first grade. Increased percentage of sight words known. Decoding skills are targeted and emerging.	All sight words are introduced. c-v-c word patterns including nonsense words are internalized and mastered. c-c-v-c word patters are introduced and targeted (e.g., clip, flat, trip, crib). c-c-v-c-c word patterns are introduced after the patterns above are mastered (e.g., crunch, stomp, fresh, plant). Use of nonsense words to practice decoding patterns.	All multisensory programs noted earlier would be appropriate.

	INSTRUCTIONAL GOALS	COMMON PROGRAMS
Early Stage II Typically corresponds to the first half of second grade. All word patterns previously taught are fully mastered. Sight words mastered automatically. Decoding skills broadened.	Two-syllable word patterns with short vowels introduced (e.g., combat, tidbit, batten). Fluency targeted & practiced. Comprehension/vocabulary emerging.	Multisensory reading programs.
Late Stage II Typically corresponds to middle of second to middle of third grade.	Multisyllabic words are emphasized. Fluency increased & targeted. Comprehension/vocabulary.	Chapter books and children's literature.

	INSTRUCTIONAL GOALS	COMMON PROGRAMS
Stage III Typically corresponds to third through sixth grades.	Comprehension. Vocabulary/word awareness.	Chapter books. Literature. Nonfiction, etc.
Decoding has been mastered and no longer is included in the instruction.	No decoding instruction necessary. Some fluency practice.	

Multisensory Programs

- Alphabetic Phonics: www.eps.schoolspecialty.com
- Barton Reading & Spelling System: www.BartonReading.com
- Herman Method (Revised as "New Herman Method"): www.voyagersopris.com/literacy/the-new-herman-method/overview
- Language! Live: www.voyagersopris.com
- Lindamood-Bell: www.lindamoodbell.com
- Orton-Gillingham: www.ortonacademy.org
- Slingerland: www.slingerland.org
- Project Read: www.ProjectRead.com
- Recipe for Reading: www.eps.schoolspecialty.com
- Preventing Academic Failure (PAF): www.PAFProgram.com
- Reading Horizons: www.readinghorizons.com
- S.P.I.R.E.: www.spire.org
- Wilson Language Training: www.WilsonLanguage.com

Helpful Websites

The following websites are extremely helpful in terms of providing a wealth of information on dyslexia and other learning disabilities.

- Bright Solutions for Dyslexia: www.brightsolutions.us
- The Cooper Learning Center (Dr. Selznick is the director of the Cooper Learning Center, Department of Pediatrics, Cooper University Health Care.): www.cooperlearningcenter.org
- Dyslexia Training Institute: www.dyslexiatraininginstitute.org
- International Dyslexia Association: www.interdys.org
- Learning Disabilities Association of America: www.ldaamerica.org
- Learning Ally: www.learningally.org
- National Center for Learning Disabilities: www.ncld.org
- Reading Rockets: www.readingrockets.org
- Shut-Down Learner: Dr. Selznick's website contains over 300 blog posts, videos and other updates on a regular basis. Sign up to receive his blog posts through email. www.shutdownlearner.com
- Understood: www.understood.org
- Yale Center for Dyslexia & Creativity: www.dyslexia.yale.edu

Staying in Touch with Dr. Selznick

To receive news, updates & blogs, visit Dr. Selznick's website, www.shutdownlearner.com.

To follow Dr. Selznick on Twitter, go to www.twitter.com/DrSelz.

Join "The Shut-Down Learner" on Facebook as a community page and click "Like." www.facebook.com/DrSelz.

To follow Dr. Selznick on LinkedIn, go to ww.linked.com/in/richardselznick.

You can also reach Dr. Selznick through email: rselznick615@gmail.com.

Books by Dr. Selznick

To receive personalized signed copies of Dr. Selznick's books and to bulk order for schools and parenting groups, go to www.shutdownlearner.com.

The Shut-Down Learner: Helping Your Academically Discouraged Child (2009), Richard Selznick, Ph.D., Sentient Publications (ISBN: 978-1-59181-078-0)

School Struggles: A Guide to Your Shut-Down Learner's Success (2012), Richard Selznick, Ph.D., Sentient Publications (ISBN: 978-1-59181-178-7)

Dyslexia Screening: Essential Concepts for Schools & Parents, (2015) Richard Selznick, Ph.D. SDL Consulting & Publishing (ISBN: 978-1-6319258-9-4)

What to Do About Dyslexia: 25 Essential Points for Parents, (2019) Richard Selznick, Ph.D., Sentient Publications (ISBN: 978-1-59181-300-2)

ACKNOWLEDGMENTS

As a psychologist, my mission has been to help smooth the road for struggling children and their parents. A significant percentage of these children struggle, for a variety of reasons, with developing adequate reading, spelling, and writing skills.

Unlike, say, the field of dentistry, where there is agreement among practitioners about how to diagnose and treat, there's no exact path that those of us who work with dyslexic children follow, and for me it's always child-by-child, family-by-family. What may work for one situation may not for another.

Every child and family I have met with has enriched my experience, broadened my understanding. So, thank you to all those I have seen over the years. I hope I have made some impact.

I would like to acknowledge and thank Cooper University Health Care, particularly my colleagues in the Department of Pediatrics. I have greatly enjoyed the professionalism and spirit of collaboration among the different pediatric specialties. A special thanks to the Pediatric Division Head, Dr. Michael Goodman, for his ongoing support, encouragement, and friendship.

To the staff of the Cooper Learning Center, thank you for all your efforts over the years. I have always been incredibly impressed by the passion with which you work with each child, doing everything you can to remediate and encourage children.

In the first stage of writing this book, Stephanie Manuzek was a crack editor, helping to bring lumpy clay to its current form. I greatly appreciate and value her input as the book came to fruition.

Thanks to Jeanne Voelker, Sue Chavis, Amy Leitner, and G. Emerson Dickman for offering your comments, support and insight along the way.

A special note of recognition goes to Connie Shaw, Publisher, of Sentient Publications. I still remember her message on my voicemail back in 2008, telling me that Sentient was offering to publish my first book, *The Shut-Down Learner*. What an exciting day that was. I am so grateful for the ongoing support, professionalism, and friendship shown by Sentient and Connie throughout all these years.

Thank you to all my friends who in your own way have contributed to this book, directly and indirectly. You know who you are, and I hope you know that I greatly value and appreciate our relationship.

To my wife, Gail, and my children, Julia and Daniel, what can I say? All your love, support and, at times, a good swift kick in the rear end, has been the fuel for me to take on the endeavor of writing this book. I love you. Thank you.

ABOUT THE AUTHOR

Dr. Richard Selznick is a psychologist, nationally certified school psychologist, assistant professor of pediatrics, school consultant and Wilson certified reading instructor. As the director of the Cooper Learning Center, a division of the Department of Pediatrics at Cooper University Healthcare, he oversees a program that assesses and treats a broad range of learning and school-based behavioral problems in children.

Dr. Selznick has presented to parents and educators internationally, as far as Dubai and Abu Dhabi and throughout the United States. A down-to-earth speaker who presents complex issues in non-jargon terms, he has a particular passion for helping parents understand dyslexia and related reading disorders. He facilitates parenting groups and is called upon by local community groups to offer his understanding of parenting and raising children in the 21st century. *What to Do About Dyslexia* is his fourth book.

To learn more about Dr. Selznick, and to receive his blog, go to www.shutdownlearner.com. You can follow him on Twitter (@DrSelz) and on Facebook under The Shut-Down Learner.